Business Expert Guide Series

Business Expert Guide to

Small Business Success

Business Expert Publishing
Thomson, Georgia

Business Expert Publishing
The Business Expert Publisher™
P.O. Box 1389
Thomson, GA 30824

Published by Business Expert Publishing
Printed in the United States of America

Cover Design: Dave Blaker
Book Editors: Sharon P. Salz , Myra Salz, Carrie Blount

First Edition

ISBN-13: 9781935602040
ISBN-10: 1935602047

Foreword

By Jill Konrath

My life as a small business owner has been filled with ups and downs. I've had some incredible years working with top-notch organizations on highly profitable projects where my work really made a difference.

That's when you know that you made the right decision to go into business by yourself. I'm on one of those highs right now. My books (*Selling to Big Companies, Get Back to Work Faster and SNAP Selling*) are doing well. Clients are calling me. Life is good.

But there were a few stretches in there that were brutal. A few years back, my consulting business virtually collapsed when my two biggest customers came under pressure from Wall Street to deliver better earnings. When all unnecessary expenses were slashed from their budgets, suddenly, I had no work.

Worse yet, I couldn't figure out what direction I wanted to take my business. My traditional customer base was shifting and my own interests were changing. After several false re-starts, I was even concerned that I'd lost my mojo.

There were other times when I hired the wrong people, ended up in legal battles with former partners, and made poor strategic decisions. Sometimes it's amazing how one fairly intelligent person can do so many dumb things.

Fortunately, I've decided that there is no such thing as failure. That being said, I've been blessed with many valuable learning opportunities. Some have been painful, others costly. But all have given me a chance to discover what it takes to be successful as a small business owner.

What have I learned along the way? That other people are so much smarter than I am in just about every area. I have this little niche of expertise. But it's just one piece of what I need to know to be successful in business.

In some areas, I'm so clueless I don't even know how to ask intelligent questions. I'm often blind to the assumptions and beliefs that impact my thinking. And many times, I don't even see what's possible because of my limited experience.

Over the years, I've assembled an unofficial board of advisors who I use on a regular basis. New ones are added as needed, while others quietly disappear as I internalize what they taught me.

But here's the deal. Most of my advisors don't even know I exist. They're people who share their expertise like the co-authors of this book. I've read their newsletters, studied their articles and listened to their audio programs. I've attended their webinars and taken copious notes.

Their fresh perspectives, sage advice and keen insights have been invaluable. I've learned from their mistakes and grown from their provocative questions. Their step-by-step guidance has propelled my business to new heights and saved it from collapse. I'm eternally grateful for their contributions to my success.

Perhaps the most frustrating part of being self-taught is figuring out which experts to learn from. When you don't even know what you don't know, it's easy to make a wrong decision.

That's what I love about this book. Lee B. Salz, Founder and CEO of *Business Expert Webinars*, knows who's good. He's assembled a board of advisors for us and brought them all together in The *Business Expert Guide to Small Business Success*.

Go check out that Table of Contents right now. The answers to your most pressing questions are just waiting to be found.

Jill Konrath
Internationally recognized sales strategist
Author of *SNAP Selling and Selling to Big Companies*

Table of Contents

1 | Strategic Business Plan Design

By John W. Myrna

As management guru Peter Drucker has observed, "Management is doing things right; leadership is doing the right things." Your strategic business plan is the tool that helps you to make sure you are focused on the right things.

As another great guru, Yogi Berra, has observed, "You've got to be very careful if you don't know where you're going, because you might not get there."

Strategic planning organizes and anchors a company's investments in the future. When you make an investment you need a platform that will remain stable long enough to complete the investment and realize the reward. To deliver real results, you need a good strategic business planning process that provides the platform for making sure everything you do today is consistent with where you want to be in the future.

Business planning is a continuous process of answering three questions.

- Where are we now?

- Where do we want to be in the future?

- What do we need to focus on over the next period to get there?

Get Ready to Plan

The planning process starts with establishing the team that will develop the plan. It is unlikely that any single individual, outside expert, consultant, or even the CEO understands all the specifics of your company, market, and technology as well as the team of people who experience it day-in and day-out. Further, no outsider or single individual will execute your plan. Execution requires a committed team that understands not only *what* they are expected to do, but *why and how* they must act.

Your planning team should have five to twelve members who can look at the business like an executive; i.e. through the eyes of the CEO. (A true executive is someone who seeks answers that optimize the entire organization; not just their department, people, or own position.) The team should include the owner(s) and their direct reports, heads of major company functions, and one or two employees who will have a major impact on the future. The team can be augmented with one or two outsiders who have a major stake in the company's success. The team already possesses the knowledge needed to create the plan. If they do not have the specific answers, they can identify questions whose answers become part of the plan's execution.

The CEO is a key member of the planning team. The three responsibilities a CEO cannot delegate are leading the strategic planning process, developing the management team, and making the "you bet the company" decisions. These three responsibilities are at the heart of strategic business planning. The planning process provides an opportunity for the CEO to judge his team. By listening to everyone before giving the "correct answer," the CEO can learn just how well his team understands the issues and existing direction. Dotting the "i's" and crossing the "t's" will make sure that the plan aligns with the CEO's wishes while allowing enough room for the team to end up truly owning the final plan.

The most effective environment for creating the plan is a well-facilitated, intense two-day meeting. Disciplining yourself to complete the plan within two days keeps the team's yearly focus on implementation, the hardest part of any plan. If you can cover all the key company issues in one meeting, you and your team will generate a plan that better balances competing issues such as growth, profitability, and competition.

Let's take a look at the three key questions we started with, one by one. The planning process begins with determining where you are now.

Step 1: Where Are We Now?

To identify where your company is now, evaluate your firm's Weaknesses, Opportunities, Threats, and Strengths in what's known as the "WOTS-up" process. Conducting a WOTS-up analysis allows you to identify the major issues facing your company today, and helps the entire team gain a comprehensive understanding of those issues and possible responses.

Before your planning meeting, solicit independent thinking from your team through a structured online input form. Ask for answers to these questions:

* What are the company's five top weaknesses, opportunities, threats, strengths, and trends?

* Where do they personally want to see the company within five years, including where the major market and product focus should be?

* What parts of the status quo do they think need to change?

Soliciting prioritized input before the team gets together minimizes the risk of "group think." It also gets the team members to start thinking independently and strategically.

During the planning meeting, utilize handouts consolidated from this input and hold a facilitated discussion around each of the WOTS-up topics. This helps each team member understand everyone's perspective on the most important issues. The key value of this process is the interactive discussions that develop insights.

Document **Where you are** with a prioritized list of the dozen or so identified major issues, including a short commentary on each.

Step 2: Where Do We Want to Be in the Future?

Once you know where you stand today, you can then develop a strategy, mission, and vision for where you want your company to be in the future. Progress is accelerated by making sure that each action you take today is consistent with where you want to be within one quarter, one year, five years and beyond. Decide where you want to end up, and then work backwards to identify what you should be working on today.

Strategy is the strategic focus of your plan. Growing your company is like assembling a giant jigsaw puzzle. Imagine you and your team working on the puzzle without the picture on the box. Even worse, there are extra pieces tossed in from other puzzles. Creating, documenting, and communicating a picture of where you want to be within five years gets everybody on the same page. Comparing that picture against where you are today identifies the gaps that you need to focus on closing over the next 1½ years.

Your **Strategy** should be consistent with your **Vision** and **Mission**. Think of your **Mission** as the DNA for your organization. It is how you "genetically engineered" your company to survive and thrive in the marketplace. It creates a focus and affirmation of the company you intend to become over the next three to five years. Agree on one or two words or phrases that answer each of the following four questions:

- Who do you want to be? (Usually some statement of leadership)

- What do you want to do? (Usually some combination of develop, manufacture, supply, or market specific services or products)

- Who do you want to do it for? (Usually a statement of geographic scope, industry, targeted customer profile)

- Why do you do it? (Usually to create value for your customers, employees, and owners along with a "softer" thought like aid the environment, save lives, have fun)

The words and phrases can be "wordsmithed" into a nice paragraph after the team agrees on the content. It's the content that provides focus.

Futurist John Naisbitt has cautioned that "Strategic planning is worthless – unless there is first a strategic vision." Your **Vision** informs your **Mission**. Companies that stand the test of time are anchored with a set of three to five core values shared by all employees and a broad focusing core purpose beyond "making money." They are inspired by a Big Hairy Audacious Goal that might take ten to thirty years to achieve.

To create your **Strategy**, ask yourself and your team where you *want to be* within five years. It is important that everyone understands that they are not being asked for a forecast, projection, or prediction. Document that strategy as specific answers to the following questions:

- Revenue: how much from internally generated growth, how much from acquisitions, how much from existing clients and products, and how much from new?

- Profit: EBITDA, gross margin, pre-tax and is it before or after items such as bonuses, profit-sharing, 401(k) contributions, charitable donations, etc.?

- Acquisitions and partnerships: how many, what range of size, is it for revenue, customers, people, technology?

- Relationships: vendors, customers, competitors?

- Market focus: how many markets, descriptions, adding/dropping, what is each one's share of revenue and profit?

- Product focus: how many, descriptions, adding/dropping, what is each one's share of revenue and profit?

- Customer profiles: how many major customers, how many total customers?

- Geography: your target market, proactively seeking customers -- local, regional, national, North American, international, or global?

- Productivity: what are your productivity goals for revenue and profit per employee? How will you utilize automation, outsourcing, globalization, and re-engineering?

- Organization: number of full-time equivalent employees to support the business, major job categories, key positions to add, and staff development?

- Locations: where are HQ, new facilities, and / or remote offices?

- Technology strategy: innovator, fast follower, slow adapter, late adapter? The role of the Internet and emerging technologies?

- Branding: under the radar, larger than life, look and feel, promotion?

- Risk management: what is the largest concentration that is acceptable of customer revenue, product, and industry?

For the strategy to communicate effectively, it must include specific numbers such as "grow to $15 million with a consistent pretax margin of 12%." Vague statements such as "grow larger with a superior profit" do not work. All numbers should be estimated to the "ballpark" level of accuracy, as close as the team's current knowledge allows.

Have your team put their hand over their hearts and take the following oath: "I will never do something stupid because of something written on a sheet of paper." Why? It seems that everyone has had the experience of providing a number in good faith and subsequently being clubbed with it months later. Without the above oath, there is a fear that management will forget the context and use any specific number as a club. Taking the oath frees the team to make their strategy statement crystal clear. Here is an example of doing something stupid: An owner set the company's targets based on number of units manufactured. Month after month, people scheduled jobs with high unit counts at the expense of jobs with higher revenue and profit.

Step 3: What Do We Need to Focus On Over the Next Period to Get There?

Once you know where you are and where you want to go, you can take the third step of matching your **Strategy** against the prioritized, understood set of issues that document where you are now. Identify the most important things that must be in place within 18 months in order for the team to be on a path to realizing the strategy. In other words, strategy is simply the team's visualization of where they want to be within five years.

Identify four to six major **Goals** that group the changes in status quo required to implement and achieve the outcomes. Identify a single individual with passion and competence to champion each of the goals. The rule of thumb is simple: one **Goal** per champion. By definition, an individual can only have one most important goal. Developing the goals as a team keeps everyone on the same page. Driving implementation autocratically makes sure each goal gets priority attention.

Develop an action plan for each **Goal**. Action plans are the vehicle for managing execution and achieving the **Goals**. Action plans identify the goal, key results, champions, and accountable persons. For each **Goal**, ask the team to identify the one to seven key results that need to be in place within 12 months in order to declare success. For each key result, identify a single, named individual who is accountable for achieving that result. (Although most results will require a team of implementers, saying that "everybody" is accountable does not work.) Every goal, key result, and action step requires a single named individual who is accountable for knowing where we are, why we are there, and what we are doing about it. This use of accountability is similar to how the CFO of a company accounts for revenue the salesmen produced or the operating expenses the production department incurred.

Each named party is accountable for maintaining action steps that are actually moving toward achieving the Key Results. Action steps are bursts of activity, driven by a single named individual, with a due date within 90 days.

Putting It All Together

Planning is a process rather than an event. Once a year, set aside a couple of days with the current planning team to close out last year's plan and create this year's plan. Simply hauling out last year's plan and adding a thin new coat of shellac cannot possibly address all the changes that have taken place over the course of a year. The assumptions you built into the **Strategy** will have been tested -- some verified, others disproved. You will have identified unanticipated opportunities. Everyone on your team will have a greater understanding of the markets, products, technology, and competitive environment. The planning team – and everyone else in the market -- is a year smarter and likely has changed. Many of the company's Goals have been accomplished and become the status quo. Other **Goals** and their **Key Results** will require more focus to get implemented.

So, you must intellectually rip up last year's plan and rebuild it based on today's issues and insights. Each aspect of the plan has a different level of stability. Visualize your plan as a pyramid made up of six stable investment platforms (see The Progress Pyramid™). Tactical initiatives produce a result within days, weeks, or months. They don't require a platform that is stable beyond 90 days. Strategic investments can take years or decades before producing a return. They must have an equally long and stable platform. The strategic plan provides six investment platforms, each one stable long enough to enable a return on an investment.

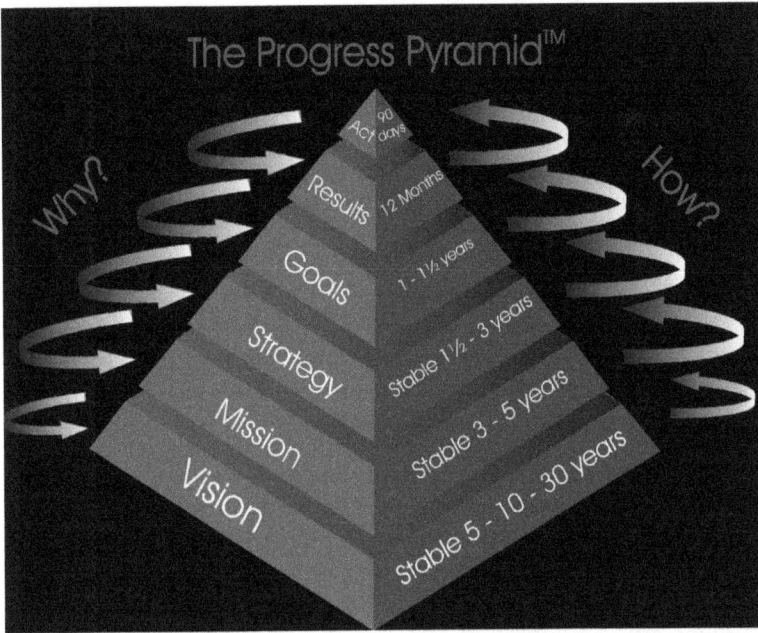

You can accelerate your progress by making sure that each action you take today is consistent with where you want to be within one quarter, one year, five years and beyond. Ask yourself: Why are you taking this particular action today? It is to produce a specific result that supports reaching a goal that implements your **Strategy**, one that is consistent with your **Mission** and **Vision**.

The **Vision** gives you a stable base for decades – five, ten, or thirty years. Your company's core values and core purpose act as an anchor and stabilizer, especially during periods of rapid change. The Big Hairy Audacious Goal (BHAG) inspires your team. Here's an example of how this might look for a hypothetical service company:

Values: Customer first, excellence, integrity

Purpose: Provide superior solutions in support of mission critical communications

BHAG: Sail though $100 million

Because **Vision** is stable for decades it does not have a lot of detail. A logical question is how to achieve it. The **Mission** provides a stable focus for three to five years, a base from which to achieve the **Vision**. It communicates to and focuses the company around an affirmation of what the company wants to be, what it wants to do, who it wants to do it for, and reminds everyone why they do it. For example:

> *To be the leading system integrator delivering mission-critical communications solutions to government agencies. Applying our expertise, resources, and technology creates a legacy and builds value for our customers, employees, and owners.*

Even with one or two paragraphs of detail, an obvious question is how the **Mission** gets achieved. The **Strategy** provides a stable focus for 1½-3 years. (The picture it paints is set five years out, but with a full page of detail in the strategic plan it evolves over a shorter time period.) **Strategy** provides the transition between the vagueness of a **Vision** and **Mission** and the specifics of **Strategic Goals** and their supporting action plans. For example, using the same hypothetical company, the strategy looks like this:

> *$20 million, internally grown, with consistent 15% EBIDA. Expand the business to include Federal, as well as local and state government agencies. Grow to 50% Federal.*

> *Support the business with under 80 employees. Develop over 10 middle managers.*

> *Diversify so no one customer represents more than 25% of our revenue.*

How do you implement your **Strategy**? How do you make real that visualization of where you want to be within three to five years? Four to six **Strategic Goals** change the company's status quo, putting it on the path to achieving its **Strategy**. What makes a goal strategic is that it will literally change the status quo, involving multiple departments and requiring a sustained commitment from the senior team. Here is how our hypothetical company's strategic goals might look. Note that each goal has a single individual assigned to it, as discussed above in Step 3.

1. *Dramatically grow sales and revenue. (Pat Hayes)*
2. *Build partnerships. (Fran Diaz)*
3. *Enhance the organization. (Chuck Griffin)*
4. *Expand our infrastructure. (Raj Cox)*

How do you actually achieve your **Strategic Goals**? Achieving the set **Key Results** for each **Strategic Goal** implements them. For example:

2. *Build partnerships. (Fran Diaz)*

2.1 *We've identified a complete set of partners to support system integration. (Jim)*

2.2 *We've identified the equipment manufacturers to complete our solution set. (Lynn)*

How do you actually achieve a **Key Result**? Executing the right **Action Steps** in the here and now, within the next 90 days, produces the **Key Results**. **Action Steps** are bursts of action sandwiched between the day-to-day operations. Each **Action Step** has a single owner and a drop-dead date for completion. For example:

2.2 *We've identified the equipment manufacturers to complete our solution set. (Lynn)*

2.2.1 *Sign re-seller contracts within 30 days. (Lynn)*

2.2.2 *Create portfolio deck within 60 days. (Dan)*

2.2.3 *Train sales team on products within 90 days. (Dan)*

Once the team decides what the company wants to accomplish, it needs to communicate it to everyone who can help make it real. Document the plan quickly, within a week of the planning meeting. Present the key aspects of the plan to the whole company. Initiate implementation immediately. (The next chapter explains how to implement your plan.)

The CEO and team need to create and own the plan. You always get a better result when the people implementing the plan have shaped it and believe in it. If you engage outside consultants to help with strategic planning, the best role for them is facilitating the planning process. Companies go through their planning process once a year, but professional planning facilitators execute a planning process every week. When the stakes are high, it pays to get the help of a professional facilitator who can take you through a proven process. Specific **Key Results** in the plan may require outside expertise. Consultants are most effective when they are targeted to deliver specific results such as research, process development, or training, etc.

The ancient Greeks loved to gamble with dice. Despite their tradition of mathematical expertise they gave identical odds to a pair of thrown dice adding up to seven or twelve. Why? Because they believed that the outcome of each throw was in the hands of the gods on Mount Olympus. It never occurred to them that they could control the overall outcome by making better-informed choices.

Strategic business planning puts the future in your hands. Making better decisions today dramatically improves your probability of future success.

Your strategic business plan is not the end of the process, it is just the beginning. As Peter Drucker reminds us, "Plans are only good intentions unless they immediately degenerate into hard work."

John W. Myrna *is a pragmatic management coach and co-founder of Myrna Associates, specializing in helping companies with $2 to $100 million in revenue create targeted and actionable strategic plans. With extensive experience in C-level and senior management positions before starting his own firm in 1991, John is an expert on the application of strategic planning. He has invested over 10,000 hours in facilitating the development and execution of hundreds of companies' strategic plans, enabling him to create and continuously refine unique solutions to typical company challenges. John is a frequent speaker and author. Reach him at johnw@myrna.com or www.myrna.com*

2 | Strategic Business Plan Implementation

By John W. Myrna

There is an old child's riddle as retold by Mark L. Feldman:

"Five frogs are sitting on a log. Four decide to jump off. How many are sitting on the log?"

The answer is five. There are five frogs left sitting on the log because there's a difference between deciding and doing.

The strategic business plan is your company's road map of what the planning team decided to do. The challenge is how to translate those decisions into doing.

There are four enablers for successful implementation. The folks you are counting on to implement the plan have to do the following:

- Understand that this is what you really want. In a busy environment where people are constantly being asked to do things, your requests must stand out.

- Believe that this is the right thing for them to prioritize and do. Dedicated employees prioritize the things they know are in the best interests of the company, not the things a sometimes clueless management asks them to.

- Know how to do it. They must have sufficient competence, time, and resources.

- Have a system that keeps them on track, captures and reflects lessons learned, and keeps them on the same page with every stakeholder.

Know It's What You Really Wanted

The written strategic business plan, understood and supported by the company's CEO and senior team, is the primary communications vehicle. The plan needs to communicate specific objectives in a crystal-clear manner. However, people pay more attention to what their leaders do than what they say. Setting deadlines, having regular follow-up, and establishing positive and negative consequences all speak louder than words. The old chestnut "what gets measured gets done" speaks to this adage. Senior managers can have a surprising impact by simply popping into someone's office and asking how things are going on their project.

A venture capitalist wondered why the company he invested in was not achieving the objectives outlined in their strategic business plan. After observing the company's president for a couple of days, he had his answer. The president was directing a steady stream of ideas, suggestions, and requests at his employees. Important and unimportant requests were all presented with identical passion and lack of follow-up. The constant flurry of hundreds of requests had became little more than noise to the staff. The company got back on track once the president focused on communicating the company's handful of strategic objectives.

Believe It's the Right Thing to Do

People resist acting when they do not see the value of the action. Corporate culture determines what is truly important. When your objectives align with employees' beliefs about what is important, the employees have no problem giving these objectives priority and implementing them. When there is misalignment, you need to shift beliefs and force a new prioritization on their part.

Consider a printing company that for decades made its profits by running big jobs for large financial institutions. Every employee knew that the way to guarantee success for the company and earn their annual bonus was to optimize big jobs. The big jobs amortized the substantial set-up and teardown costs inherent with silk screen printing. Then the market changed and the majority of available jobs were from smaller financial institutions with jobs only one-tenth the size of those from the big firms. The sales team worked to sell ten times as many jobs to keep volume up. The production people, however, were still prioritizing based on what they knew was the most profitable, i.e. big jobs. Every time the sales team brought in a new customer with a small job, the production people put it at the bottom of the queue – doing what they knew was in the best interests of the company.

Unfortunately there will not be a second job when the first job for a new customer is delivered late. In order for the printing company to implement their strategic business plan, they had to re-educate their production people so they understood that small jobs had to become as much of a priority as big jobs. They also had to support that change by investing in new equipment and processes that enabled them to run small jobs profitably.

Your measurement and compensation system must align with your strategic business plan. If your plan is to diversify the customer base, the sales commission plan needs to reward more than total revenue. Calling on new customers drops to the bottom of sales reps' to-do list when the sales team knows that the only thing that counts is meeting the monthly revenue target.

Know How to Do It

Matching a task to the people with the best mix of passion and competence is a key management skill. The people tasked with the job need to both want to do it and know how to do it. Competence can vary as much as a hundred-to-one based on aptitude and experience. An employee can gain the competence if he has exceptional passion for a task and sufficient aptitude to learn. Such a person may have to work twice as hard to get the job done, but will do so willingly because it is an opportunity for growth.

No one is sitting around waiting for something to do. Internal candidates with the competence to implement may not be available to take on a new task. This is an opportunity to review where people are spending their time. Breaking existing tasks into prioritized groups is a well-proven time-management process. Prioritization is based on the Pareto principle, which suggests that about 20 percent of our tasks deliver 80 percent of the value. It is important to prioritize tasks based on their ability to deliver value and itemize them from most significant to less significant. Review an internal candidate's current workload and assign each of that person's tasks to one of the following groups:

A. Tasks that must be done or there will be serious consequences.

B. Tasks that should be done or there will be mild consequences.

C. Tasks that would be nice to do but are without significant consequences.

D. Tasks that could be eliminated altogether without any real consequence.

Step one in making time available is eliminating or resizing C and D tasks. Step two is utilizing delegation.

Take a good look at your A and B tasks. You will always be the most productive when you are focused on the things that only you can do. The question is, what sub-tasks of your A and B tasks can only you do? You can contribute to five times as many A and B level tasks by restricting your direct involvement to the critical 20 percent of their sub-tasks and delegating the rest. Even better, if you can focus on the 20 percent of that 20 percent -- i.e., the most critical 4 percent of an A or B task -- you can increase your impact by another factor of five. This allows you to be 25 times more impactful than if you performed the entire task yourself.

Consider a manufacturer that specialized in point-of-sale displays. The CEO and Sales Director struggled to recruit sales reps. Not only was their market specialized, but also it took months for anyone new to fully master the company's complex product line. They asked their sales reps how many hours a week were actually spent selling, and the answer was a startling 10 hours. The other hours were spent following up on sales, filling out paperwork for orders, making sure the plant correctly completed the job, and generating reports. Adding another sales rep would add only another ten hours a week of selling.

The company took an alternative approach to hiring. They identified an employee who could relate to both the sales reps and the plant personnel. With training and coaching, the employee was able to assume responsibility for managing the relationships with the plant, taking it off the sales reps' plate. By further streamlining the order entry and reporting functions, each sales rep doubled their selling time. This had the immediate effect of more than doubling the effectiveness of the sales force, all without having to recruit and train any new sales reps! This approach can resolve bottlenecks in sales, product development, and engineering -- all hard-to-recruit positions with major impact that require a very specialized skill.

Leveraging your high-priced talent is a key strategy for increasing profitability. If you do not have existing staff with the right mix, you must get it from the outside. Delegation enables you to utilize less expensive, junior people when you are ready to hire. Since each new hire has a significant impact on your break-even point, hiring should be your last choice. If the task is to develop a process or system, the best approach is to hire a consultant or independent contractor with the core competence to build the initial version. Once the system or process is developed, you assign or hire full-time staff to run and maintain it. Developing a system or process requires different, and usually more expensive skills than running, expanding, and maintaining one.

Have a System to Follow

Implementation is a four-step cycle of agreement, accountability, action, and assessment (see The Progress Accelerator™). Creating a virtuous cycle accelerates implementation while reducing the waste and quality hits that come with poor communications.

1. *Agreement* is the first phase in the cycle. It is necessary to agree on the priority of issues, tactical approach, and expected outcomes among the appropriate stakeholders. At a strategic level, this agreement is best reached between the CEO and the senior team during a two-day planning meeting and documented in the strategic plan. At a tactical level, reaching this agreement can be as simple as the huddle football players hold before every play.

To implement, you need consensus and commitment from the implementers. Consensus is reached when every member of the implementation team agrees that the implementation plan makes sense. It may not be exactly what they would do if it was up to them exclusively, but it makes sense for the company. If it does not make

The Progress Accelerator™

sense for the company, then they need to keep working on the plan until it does. Commitment comes from a belief that this task is worth doing.

Real consensus and commitment are achieved when the implementation team members have voiced and worked through their concerns and misgivings prior to a team decision that all will support in public. Commitment is achieved through four stages:

• Trust within a team enables people to be open.

• When people are open, they express their doubts and misgivings.

- When they express and have worked through their doubts and misgivings, they feel they were party to the final decision.

- When they feel party to the decision, they can commit to it.

  Execution is all but impossible unless team members commit to the implementation plan.

2. *Accountability* refers to personal accountability or responsibility for completing a task and producing the agreed-upon outcome. Whether for a tactical action step or a key result measure, one (and only one) person must be designated to be accountable. There will always be multiple people involved, but without a single point of accountability you get the situation that correspondent Charles Osgood related in "A poem about responsibility." He recounted an old story about four people named Everybody, Somebody, Anybody, and Nobody (paraphrased below):

   > *There was an important job to be done and Everybody was sure Somebody would do it. Anybody could have done it, but Nobody did it. Somebody got angry about that, because it was Everybody's job. Everybody thought Anybody could do it, but Nobody realized that Everybody wouldn't do it. It ended up that Everybody blamed Somebody when Nobody did what Anybody could have done.*

3. *Action* is tactical. It is a burst of activity that moves us closer to the desired outcome. One person is personally accountable for making sure it happens within a specified time period. Texas Instruments called this the W3 model:

- What will get done – a burst of activity that moves us closer to the objective

- Who will be accountable to make it happen – the catalyst and record keeper

- When will it be completed – the drop-dead date for completion

   As Alec Mackenzie said in *The Time Trap*, his classic book on time management, *"A goal without a deadline is just a dream."*

   Ninety days is the window for tactical action. Focusing on the actions that will actually get done this week, this month, and this quarter keeps execution real.

4. *Assessment* is accomplished in a review meeting. Tactical actions can be assessed during a daily, weekly, or monthly huddle that starts with a question about what we may have learned about previous plays, weak spots, etc. Strategically, senior management needs to close out the year's strategic goals during an annual two-day meeting. Closing last year's goals requires that management identify where the status quo has actually changed, and evaluate the success at achieving goals.

   A company in the pharmaceutical market had a core business of performing one-time development work. The backlog of business was never more than 90 days. In their strategic business plan, they set a goal to obtain recurring business to mitigate year-to-year revenue volatility. In a quarterly review meeting, the sales manager shared that he was delaying his proposal to win a big recurring contract because manufacturing was very busy. There was much discussion about the myriad of issues that would have to be dealt with to win and deliver on the contract. It was clear that the current approach was not going to succeed. The team shifted into crisis mode and identified the company's biggest challenges. Each challenge had a single accountable owner and drop-dead date for completion. The president established a short meeting to be held at the start and end of every day to make sure that everything possible was being done to win. In the end, the company won the contract and successfully manufactured the new product. The company changed the status quo, shifting to a path that held the promise of reduced volatility.

Final Thoughts on Implementing

The secret of success is dealing with the twin challenges of focus and communications. Excellent implementation starts with a focus on the right things. The right things hold excellent answers to the following four questions:

- Is it real?
- Can we do it?
- Can we win?
- Is it worth it?

Picking a handful of the right things to focus on is 50 percent of success. The other 50 percent comes from ongoing, effective communications. Regular, well-facilitated meetings allow stakeholders to share lessons learned, let the company utilize their wisdom, and keep everybody on the same page with the same expectations.

The challenges of focus and communication will never be "solved." They are ongoing challenges that require a continuous process and constant vigilance. To return to the riddle we started with, once four of the five frogs have moved from deciding to doing, only one frog will be left sitting on the log. Implementation of your strategic business plan will help your company shift from deciding to do something to actually doing it, thus setting the stage for success.

John W. Myrna is a pragmatic management coach and co-founder of Myrna Associates, specializing in helping companies with $2 to $100 million in revenue create targeted and actionable strategic plans. With extensive experience in C-level and senior management positions before starting his own firm in 1991, John is an expert on the application of strategic planning. He has invested over 10,000 hours in facilitating the development and execution of hundreds of companies' strategic plans, enabling him to create and continuously refine unique solutions to typical company challenges. John is a frequent speaker and author. Reach him at johnw@myrna.com or www.myrna.com.

3 | Pricing for Profitability

Are You Priced Right?

By Sarah Day

Managing a small enterprise requires making decisions every single day – from the day you decide to open for business to the day you exit – with what sometimes seems like very little information. One of these decisions is what to charge for products and services. Pricing is a big decision on its own merits. But pricing also interacts with many other aspects of the business – inventory management, marketing spend, job costing, and many other fundamental areas. Each aspect impacts the other.

Many small businesses struggle with pricing. More often than not the focus is on being competitive and earning revenue, but rarely is the focus on overall profitability and the role that pricing plays in the business' overall growth.

We have all heard the adage, "If you are losing money on your product, you can't make up the difference in volume." Each sale of a product unit that costs you money, or each occurrence of a service where you do not make any profit impacts your overall business health. How you price your products and services can be the key factor in determining your overall business profitability.

In this chapter, we will discuss the impact of pricing and other factors on profitability, how emotions come into play, ways to assess whether pricing is suitable, and ways to determine the flexibility to take a price increase. We will also discuss special considerations for service businesses who are often trying to price their offerings based on intangible elements.

The Impact of the Right Price

In addition to impacting business revenue and bottom line profit, the right price can help your small business:

- Carve out a market position
- Manage productivity

Carving out a Market Position

The price you select for your products or services helps customers see where you fit in the market in relation to your competition. A low price may indicate that you have a value-priced or generic product. A high price might indicate a higher level of accompanying service or higher quality. The temptation in a new business is to price low to enter the market with the hopes of raising prices later. But this can set a trap for the business owner!

When you set a price you are telling the market what the product is "worth." If you set a baseline price that's too low:

- It may be difficult to justify a later increase without adding services and features.

- You could lose market share among buyers who equate higher price with higher quality, particularly if you sell to an affluent market.

- Many people, when faced with multiple bids, do not pick the lowest one! A bid that's too low could imply you have less knowledge about a project or client need.

Managing Productivity

Economic theory tells us that a lower price will result in a higher level of sales. And everyone wants a higher level of sales! However, a small business – particularly one that provides services – can be strained by sales that grow beyond their ability to provide timely, quality service. Under the right circumstances, taking a price increase can provide a huge relief in a busy, small business environment. Consider the following simple example:

Example: A small service business with $100,000 in annual revenue serving an average of 250 clients per year. Let's assume they charge $100 per client visit and service clients on average 4 times per year:

250 clients x $100 per service visit x 4 visits per year = $100,000

250 clients x 4 visits per year = 1000 client visits

Now let's say this company decides to take a 25% price increase. It's a steep increase and they will probably lose some clients, but as the equation below shows, even if they lose 20% of their clients they can still come out ahead:

200 clients x $125 per service visit x 4 visits per year = $100,000

200 clients x 4 visits per year = 800 client visits

They are earning the same amount of revenue serving fewer clients and decreasing the number of client visits per year by 20%!

What You Need to Set the Right Price

Often, failure to set the right price results from a lack of analysis or basic information. Small business owners are busy. There is always too much to do and someone waiting for a return phone call. But sometimes, that inability to get to the basic information can put you in a profitability hole. In order to get insight into your profitability and pricing you should identify some key information:

Unit cost

Charge more than it costs to make – and sell – your product. Of course you want to make sure you have covered your materials' costs in the cost of your product. But too often small businesses forget the softer costs of selling product like sales commissions, returns, or supplier discounts. When you figure the gross margin needed to cover your income and overhead, don't forget to include all the costs of getting your product to market.

Typically as the volume of your product sales grows you will be able to source larger, discounted quantities or materials or find other sources of production which should strengthen product margins. But make sure as you do this, you do not erode the quality.

Job costing

If you are not currently measuring profitability on your jobs this would be a great place to start. Pick your past five jobs (or 10...or 20, whatever number is meaningful to your business) and start there.

To measure the margin on each job:

Revenue on job

Less the cost of doing business

Less the marketing cost

Less any payments to subcontractors

Less the cost of materials

= Gross Margin (before overhead)

When you compare the results, look for patterns and profit leaks that might emerge.

Patterns. Some of the patterns you might identify will indicate higher or lower margins based on:

- Type of customer served
- Size of customer served
- Type of job performed
- Type of product sold
- Geographic area where a product is shipped
- Shipping method used
- Geographic area where a service is performed
- Frequency of service calls to customer
- Subcontractor used

Profit leaks. In a product-based business, profit leaks tend to be found in rising costs for materials, transportation and shipping or labor – things that are easily analyzed. In a service business these are less tangible and usually represent time spent. Some common profit leaks in a service business:

- Shopping for materials during the bid process rather than after the job is secured
- Strategy development not charged to customer
- Project design not charged to customer
- Project management time not built in to cost
- Unrecoverable travel time
- Return trips to correct customer problems
- Unrecoverable labor or materials provided to correct service problems

Break-even

Break-even is the point at which the revenue generated on the product that you sell equals the cost to produce or purchase the product for resale plus the associated costs to sell the product. This number can be very useful – it can help you set your marketing budget, sales compensation, or selling price as well as help you monitor your profitability.

Here's one way to calculate a simple break-even:

1. Calculate the total overhead of your business – that is, the total cost you would incur in a month regardless of whether you sold a single item. Your rent, utilities, payroll expenses, and marketing are a few of the larger expense categories you should consider.

2. If you purchase your inventory, identify the unit cost by adding the expense you incur to acquire one unit to any related costs like freight.

3. If you manufacture your inventory, identify the unit cost by adding the direct materials (including freight and related charges) to the labor it takes to build one unit. (If this is a complex equation, seek help from your accountant or another qualified professional. This number can help you assess numerous aspects of your business.)

4. Finally, calculate the profit on one unit by subtracting the total amount of expense to sell one unit from an average unit price.

5. Divide your total overhead by the profit on one unit to get the number of units you must sell to break even.

Product Margin

When the bottom line looks decent it is not unusual to put off analysis – after all, what's the point of investing time in analysis if you're making a profit?

What this approach will not tell you is whether that bottom line could be healthier, and whether there are items in your inventory that are draining away profit. A regular review of each product's profitability can help you tune your product offerings, identify your best sellers, and strengthen your financial position.

Start your analysis by calculating the margin for each individual product. This can go a long way toward identifying products that are contributing little or nothing to the bottom line:

1. If you purchase your inventory, identify the unit cost by adding the expense you incur to acquire one unit to any related costs like freight.

2. If you manufacture your inventory, identify the unit cost by adding the direct materials (including freight and related charges) to the labor it takes to build one unit. If this is a complex equation, seek help from your accountant or another financial professional.

3. Subtract the unit cost from an average sales price per unit to get the margin per unit. Why use an average sales price? If you do any discounting or volume price breaks, using the list price can significantly overstate your unit margin.

4. Divide the gross profit per unit by the average sales price to generate a margin %:

    $4.00 gross profit per unit / $49.00 sales price = 8% margin

Once you've identified the margins, compare the results to identify those products that contribute the most, or the least, on a per unit basis.

Contribution to Revenue

The product margin is an important figure to know, but it should be viewed in relation to sales volume. You may not want to cut a product that produces only a 5% margin if it represents 60% of your sales! The next step in the process is to break down your sales by product to see which products represent the biggest percentage of your revenue:

Revenue for Product A/Total Revenue

= Product A's % contribution to the total

Why Emotion in Pricing Decisions?

Pricing in a small business often has an emotional element. The identity of the business is closely tied to the owner's identity, reputation, and sense of self worth. This is especially true in service businesses where the owner may be directly representing the service to customers but is also true in product businesses where the owner may have an attachment to the product offered.

This tie can be a negative factor in setting price. What may seem like a rational decision can be hampered by strong emotions like stress, doubt, and fear. In fact, emotion can present a bigger obstacle than any market related force! These emotions arise because of:

- Fear of asking for more money
- Fear of losing a competitive pricing advantage
- Fear of losing customers
- Doubt that the services are worth what is being asked

Finally, sometimes businesses price too low out of a desperation to do business, particularly in a new business where the attitude is to start out low and raise prices later. This rarely works in practice and can seriously erode profitability over time.

If you find you are fighting emotions in your pricing decisions compromise with yourself. Raise some prices. Raise prices for some clients or products. Increase the costs of delivery or shipping. Start small and see what happens. Worst case – it confirms your fears and you can roll the pricing back. Best case – no one notices and you inch your profitability upward.

Flexibility in Pricing

There are times when you know you have to raise prices but fear can prevent you from doing so. In order to neutralize some of that fear – so you can make a rational, rather than emotional decision – try asking yourself these questions in relation to your pricing:

- *What is your closing percentage?* The greater the percentage of business you close the greater the flexibility you have with pricing. If you're consistently closing nearly 100% of your business you should definitely consider a price increase. Practically speaking, the probability of closing this much business on a consistent basis is pretty high. If you are closing at this rate it is likely you are priced quite favorably compared to your competition.

- *Are you at full capacity?* The closer you are to full capacity the more flexibility you have in raising prices. This is the simple law of supply and demand in action – the higher the demand for your product or service, the more you can charge. Of course taking a price increase may erode your client base a little but it may be that a worst case scenario is you end up doing the same amount of business with fewer clients – a welcome relief for many overloaded entrepreneurs.

- *How much of your business is repeat?* If you have little or no repeat business you have more flexibility to raise prices. While your customers will still compare your prices to those of your competitors they will not have any context by which to judge whether or not you've raised your prices.

- *What's the environment?* Economic conditions fluctuate. You should consider the current state of your market when considering a price increase. Even in a down economy some areas prosper. But if your clients are truly strained, then it is not a time to consider an increase.

- *When did you last take a price increase?* Most service business-es in particular take a regular price increase. For example, if you regularly visit a salon to have your hair cut, you are prob-ably accustomed to a price increase every 12 – 18 months.

- *What is your competition charging?* Competition is just one factor in setting prices. You should determine if you are priced significantly above or significantly below your competition. If their pricing information is not readily available, assess it by asking your customers and contacts, reviewing their advertis-ing, or by shopping for the product or service yourself.

Special Considerations for Service Businesses

Service businesses struggle with many of the same issues but they also have some unique considerations.

Deploying Subcontractors

If you are a service provider in your business, there may be times you find it necessary to bring on subcontractors to help you meet the demand for your services. If mismanaged, this can lead to a situation where everyone except the business owner is making money – the subcontractors get paid but there is nothing left for the business owner. To help combat this, figure out your daily break-even, that is, the number of hours per day you must personally bill to cover your costs (including overhead) and what you want to pay yourself:

Total monthly costs/rate per hour = number of total hours needed

Number of total hours/22 days = average daily hours to bill

Then at a minimum, cover the average daily hours needed yourself. For anything over and above that number you can deploy a subcontractor as necessary without threatening your livelihood.

"Flat" pay rates

This is a scenario often seen when a sole owner/operator finds it necessary to hire others to perform the same service that they do to free up their time for management tasks. It's not uncommon for business owners to charge the same hourly rate for these employees that they charge for themselves. This makes it hard to transition customers – after all, if your customer can work with you or your employee for the same rate why wouldn't they choose the business owner and "expert"? If you hire people in under you, raise your personal rate and give your customers a choice – they can continue to work with you and pay the higher rate or they can transition to the new employee and maintain the lower rate.

Value pricing

Most service providers, when they are starting out, base their proposals or project fees on an hourly rate. But over time they sometimes realize they are earning less than their competitors even when those competitors are less experienced! What sometimes occurs is that over time, these professionals get more proficient at their work. They can do the same high quality work in less time. Many continue to charge the same hourly rate but propose fewer hours giving their customers a bargain price for their high quality service. This is particularly true in creative professions like design and copywriting.

To combat this dilemma, think in terms of "value pricing" for your projects. Whatever your customer will pay your higher-priced competitors, they will also pay you. Price the job at a project rate rather than an hourly rate based on what they should be willing and able to pay for the worked performed. As a seasoned professional, you should be able to assess that project rate.

Conclusion

In this chapter, we discussed the impact that pricing and other factors have on profitability. We looked at ways to assess whether you are priced right, and ways to determine whether you have the flexibility to raise prices. We discussed how emotions like doubt, fear, and desperation can cloud your decision making; as well as special considerations for service businesses who are often trying to price their offerings based on intangible elements.

The tools for analysis discussed here will not only help you set pricing, but can help you with the tough decisions you make every day, like how to manage your inventory, what to spend on marketing, or how much to pay in sales commissions. Managed together, these measures can set you on a path to higher profitability.

Sarah Day is president of Day One Business Services and a growth strategist for small to medium sized enterprises. Sarah helps small business owners make management decisions including what to charge for their products and services. Using a wealth of management experience garnered during a 25-career, she helps them identify goals, key financial issues, and other areas of concern and manage their pricing to ensure overall business profitability. Sarah is also an accredited executive associate of the Institute for Independent Business, a nonprofit research, training, and accreditation organization devoted to helping small business.

4 | Managing Cash Flow

Avoiding the Financial Pitfalls

By Paul C. Pershes

As a professor of forensic accounting and forty years as a successful CPA, my expertise has provided me the answers to the most frequently asked questions. Why is one business successful and another not? Why is one individual successful in business and another not? Although there are many reasons and rationales to explain successes and failures – it is really not a mystery. Sometimes a business fails for no other reason than the business model was wrong. In several occasions, the most successful business fails because of timing ... it was started or was acquired at the wrong time. In other circumstances, the wrong location was chosen for the right business. Frequently, a new business owner just needed help from others but didn't ask for it. In my experience, many successful business people were unsuccessful in their initial business venture and only triumphed when they learned from their failures.

There are many guidelines written for starting businesses in almost any business book; however, the following are my three essential rules that will help ensure continued success:

1. Know the business and industry.
2. Make sure you have enough cash or access to financial resources for the business and personal expenses.

3.   Have the commitment and perseverance to stay with the business in difficult times – every business entrepreneur is tested with challenges throughout the life of a business.

Every new business started out as a successful business. The new owner was excited, dedicated, had tremendous drive to succeed, planned to go into business for a long time, and had the support of family and friends. How could such a formula miss? Why do so many new businesses fail?

Why do I title this chapter *"The Pitfall of a Successful Business – Managing Cash Flow?"* Every prospective business owner believes that he or she has a successful business idea or can buy a business that will make them rich. They are 100% positive they will be a better owner, the business will be profitable, and in many cases make them independently wealthy. These successful businesses can include an existing or new business franchise, an existing profitable business or the successful long running family business that will be turned over to the next generation. How can any of these businesses fail? As mentioned above, there are three essential business rules to follow to ensure business success.

This chapter focuses on **Rule 2--Have Enough Cash**. The business rule that must be followed for every business, new or existing, and the most overlooked Pitfall is … **poor management of cash flow**. Without proper cash flow … your business will fail. Managing cash flow includes not having sufficient cash to invest in the business from the start and then managing operating cash flow wisely throughout the life of the business.

Cash Flow has several components that each business owner must understand.

1.   **Initial cash investment** is the funds necessary to purchase or start up the business. This includes the purchase price of a franchise or existing business and the costs for starting up a new business.

2.   **Cash on hand and working capital** includes initial funds needed to start or purchase a business plus the funds necessary to operate the business. Working capital also includes additional funds necessary for the growth of the business.

3. **Cash available for staying power** are additional funds required for slow periods, a recession and increased competition. These funds are necessary to "Weather the Storm."

4. **Cash available for emergencies** is required to take care of the totally unexpected. The loss of a major customer or the owner getting sick – the unknown will always happen.

5. **Cash available for personal expenses** represents living expenses of the business owner and family. The last thing the new business owner wants to worry about is paying the everyday living expenses for the family. The business owner cannot be successful and concentrate on building the business if he cannot support his family.

In addition to the above listed cash flow components, there are several key accounting terms every successful business owner should have front of mind.

Operating Cash Flow represents the actual cash received during the course of the business year from sales of products and services less the actual cash disbursed for the purchase of products and services and selling, general and administrative expenses incurred during the year. The difference between cash received less cash disbursed represents Operating Cash Flow or Operating Cash Income.

Owner's Compensation represents all business and personal expenses that the business pays on behalf of the owner, including salaries and benefits, distributions and personal expenses.

Cash Basis of Accounting accounts for cash transactions only – sales that are actually received in cash and expenses that are actually paid. Income earned but not received in cash and expenses incurred although not paid are not included.

Accrual Basis of Accounting accounts for all transactions – income earned whether received in cash or not and expenses incurred whether paid or not. The accrual basis of accounting provides a more accurate method of accounting than the cash basis of accounting. The accrual basis of accounting requires accounting for all transactions as they happen whether or not you pay for them. It follows a basic accounting theory - MATCH YOUR INCOME AND EXPENSES AS THEY OCCUR. A major Pitfall of a successful business is not paying your bills timely and not understanding the accrual method of accounting.

Many small Mom and Pop businesses operate on a cash basis. They know at the end of the day how much cash they have on hand, what cash they need to pay current bills and how much they can take out for owner's compensation. A cash business is a relatively simple business and works as long as income and expense items are received and paid on a current basis. Customers pay in cash and expenses are paid regularly. Remember CASH FLOW IS NOT CASH INCOME. You may have positive cash flow for a period of time only to be SURPRISED when you cannot pay your bills.

The New Business Startup

There are hundreds of thousands of businesses that start up each year. Many people want to work for themselves. There are those that have lost their jobs and will start or buy a business to create a job; and there are those entrepreneurs that have developed a new product or business idea and want to start a business. All are very important to the American Way of Life and the success of the American Entrepreneur.

It is essential for a business owner to grasp the "rules of thumb" to owning a business.

1. Have cash for at least two years of operations – budget conservatively.

2. Make sure there are sufficient savings to cover family living costs for eighteen months – make a sound family budget that will work.

3. Make sure your family and close relatives understand the
    sacrifices that will be made during the early years of the new
    business.

The new business can be profitable in the early years but pro-
vide little or no cash flow as the business requires all available cash
for operations for the first several years. THE PRESSURE OF NOT
PAYING YOUR MORTGAGE OR RENT AND FAMILY EXPENSES
CAN EXERT ENOUGH STRAIN ON A FAMILY RELATIONSHIP
TO CAUSE THE BUSINESS TO FAIL and possibly the FAMILY.

Buying a Business Has It's Pros and Cons

Buying a business requires investing a significantly greater amount
of cash initially than starting a new business. The seller must be
paid for their years of effort, the existing assets and customers, and
the profits and business goodwill created. These assets being purchased are generally represented in a purchase price of the business of (3-4) times income before interest, taxes and depreciation
and amortization (EBITDA or positive cash flow). Generally, when
a business is sold, the seller will keep the cash on hand, accounts
receivable, real estate and retain the liabilities. Inventories are generally included in the sale price but the seller will try to reduce the
level of inventories at the time of sale. The Pitfall here is to recognize the cash needed to operate the business being acquired at
the current expected sales level. The new owner will have to add
operating cash, fund the business for the lack of existing accounts
receivable and the need for increased inventory levels to offset the
working capital taken out by the seller. This does not include the
additional cash necessary to grow the business. These hidden cash
needs often go unnoticed by the new unsophisticated buyer.

Helpful Hints

When buying a small business, negotiate to include in the purchase
price, the accounts receivable and a normal to higher amount of
inventory on hand. You may have to pay a higher purchase price

but can usually get the seller to finance a portion of the higher purchase price; thereby giving you some working capital and time to develop a business track record for future bank financing.

It is also very important to hire competent legal and financial advisors. A good attorney drafting an appropriate purchase contract with all representation and warranties from the seller will save you more money in the long run than it costs. A good CPA will be invaluable in both assisting in the negotiations of the purchase of the business and for many years thereafter. A new entrepreneur needs a financial advisor and confidant to talk to during the course of the year. The CPA would provide that role (as an outside CFO). Don't be penny wise and dollar foolish. It you cannot afford good legal and financial advice, you probably should not go into business for yourself.

Some Stories...Lessons Learned

I have helped many business owners succeed and I have had several business owners come to my door too late for rescuing. The following three stories will show how cash flow affects business ... it can crush your dream or make you a successful business owner. You will also learn that by taking a few simple steps prior to emptying your life-savings, you can avoid misfortune.

How to Lose your Life Savings in 180 Days

Mr. Hard Worker, an average individual, decided to go into business for himself. Mr. Hard Worker went to a business broker to find a business for himself and told the broker he had $100,000 in cash to invest – his life's savings. The business broker (not an attorney or financial advisor) showed Mr. Hard Worker the businesses he had available for sale that could be bought with $100,000. As rule of thumb, a small business sells for approximately (3) times owner's compensation (which includes salary, benefits, car, insurance and other personal expenses). Therefore, the purchase price of this $100,000 business would presume the owner's compensation would be $33,000.

Mr. Hard Worker engaged my CPA services just after purchasing the business. He told me that he found the expected cash flow available for owner's compensation and running the business was inadequate. He asked me what was wrong – did the seller make misrepresentations? Were the financial statements shown to him inaccurate? The business was failing and he just purchased the business. He nervously pleaded, "Help!" What was wrong? First, there was no initial cash to invest in the business. Mr. Hard Worker, now Mr. New Owner, needed cash to operate and to support the operations with initial cash and until new accounts receivable were earned and then collected – more time required and additional cash investment needed for working capital – he did not anticipate this additional investment. Second, as a new business owner, vendors wanted to be paid immediately – they did not know Mr. New Owner – another drain on working capital. Mr. Hard Worker did not have any more cash for working capital and he also needed to take money out of the business to survive. The result – within 180 days the business was failing after years of prior success.

How could Mr. Hard Worker done things differently? Mr. Hard Worker should have engaged good legal and financial advice before purchasing the business. They would have advised Mr. Hard Worker of these initial working capital cash needs once buying the business and negotiated a partial payout of the purchase price to provide the necessary initial working capital. If terms could not have been negotiated, Mr. Hard Worker should never have bought the business. His life's savings was gone … in six months.

Knowledge is Power and Business Success

Mr. Smart Worker saved $400,000 to buy a business. He was new to buying a business and sought out both legal and accounting advice. Mr. Smart Worker asked his CPA to review the financial statements of the business he wanted to buy - make recommendations as to the accuracy of the financial statements and the initial cash and working capital needs. The CPA was also asked to estimate the owner's compensation that could be withdrawn in the first year based on the prior financial statements and projections being made for the business. Mr. Smart Worker needed $100,000 in annual owner's compensation. The purchase price would generally be between $300,000 and $400,000. Most sellers want all or most of the purchase price up front.

The same Pitfalls for cash and working capital needs would result if Mr. Smart Worker did not have additional cash to invest or alternative financing sources to cover the initial cash and working capital needs described above – only in larger amounts. The CPA also advised Mr. Smart Worker that he estimated $75,000 to $100,000 would be needed in initial cash to meet the working capital needs in the first year.

Mr. Smart Worker, together with legal and financial advisors, negotiated a $250,000 down payment and a three year payout for the $150,000 balance for the remaining purchase price, thereby allowing Mr. Smart Worker, and now Mr. Successful Businessperson, to have sufficient cash and working capital to have a successful business and pay expected owner's compensation.

The Successful Business That Failed

This company, until recently, was very successful - worth over $1 billion with outstanding positive cash flow -- what went wrong? Initially, Mr. Successful Owner did everything right. He purchased prime real estate at relatively low prices, upgraded the properties as necessary and was able to increase rents. Financing was available and obtained at favorable rates and rents were continually increased to pay the additional financing costs. Cash flow continued to increase. As the fair market values of the properties increased, Mr. Successful Owner refinanced the properties and took out more cash. What could be better? NOTHING! What went wrong? - EVERYTHING!

Mr. Successful Owner started using the cash proceeds from the refinancing to invest in riskier assets at a time when the market was at the top - construction costs, prices and demand. What he did not recognize (for lack of experience) was that the market was topping out and too many new construction projects were coming into the market for sale at the same time as his. The market was declining and the ability to obtain financing by buyers was drying up. In addition, the success of prior years provided a very wealthy life style for Mr. Successful Owner as he had spent millions of dollars in owner's compensation and very expensive personal "Toys" – airplanes, homes, cars, hobbies and art.

Today, there is little equity left in the business. The "Toys" are being sold, and current cash flow is not sufficient to pay outstanding debt. What happened? It was like a Perfect Storm – the liquidity crisis hit – real estate values went down – buyers disappeared – expenses continued to increase – and there was no Staying Power or Emergency Funds. Also, Mr. Successful Owner did not recognize how the market could change so quickly. He did not set-up emergency funds during the good times to protect the investments to get him through the downturn.

Mr. Successful Owner also made mistakes by not retaining qualified legal and financial advisors. Today, Mr. Successful Owner is fighting to survive. You should never be in this position. A successful business owner prepares for the business cycles, including the unexpected downturns, hard-hitting competition, and mismanagement of cash-flow.

In summary, follow my three essential rules and you will be a successful business owner.

1. Know the business and industry you want to get into-- work in the same type of business and industry before going into your own business.

2. Make sure you have enough cash or access to financial resources for the business and personal expenses. Have the proper cash to purchase and operate your new business for at least two years.

3. Have the commitment and perseverance to stay with the business in difficult times – every business entrepreneur is tested with challenges throughout the life of a business.

Paul C. Pershes *is currently the President of Pershes & Company, P.A., providing forensic accounting, fraud, investigations, lost profit and damage calculations and business valuation services. He has more than 40 years extensive knowledge in P&L management, sales and marketing, productivity, strategic goal setting and mergers & acquisitions for public and family-owned businesses. Mr. Pershes is an adjunct Professor at Baruch College teaching Forensic Accounting. He is a Certified Public Accountant in both New York and Florida; a Certified Valuation Analyst (CVA); a Certified Financial Analyst (CFF) and Accredited in Business Valuations (ABV). Paul can be reached at ppershes@aol.com.*

5 | Strategic Decision-Making

The Essential Leadership Skill

By Joseph Riggio, Ph.D.

What Is Strategic Decision-Making?

Let's take a look at what most people think about when they think about decision-making, and how that relates to the needs of business leaders.

One of the most dramatic and highly documented examples of decision-making in recent history was the controlled ditching of US Airways Flight 1549 by Captain Chesley "Sully" Sullenberger in the Hudson River.

This flight was scheduled to go from LaGuardia Airport in New York City (NY) to Seattle Tacoma International Airport (WA), with a stopover in Charlotte/Douglas International Airport (NC). However, on its initial climb off the runway at LaGuardia, just two minutes after take-off, the aircraft collided with a flock of Canadian Geese. Both engines (left and right) ingested birds and failed, causing the aircraft to lose all thrust. At this point the aircraft was going down.

When the collision took place the co-pilot, First Officer Jeffrey B. Skiles, was at the controls. Immediately, Captain Sullenberger took over and began to pilot the aircraft. At this point Skiles, as co-pilot, began seeking ways to restart the engines ... ultimately to no avail. Within thirty seconds of taking over from the co-pilot, Captain Sullenberger announced to the air control tower that he would be returning to LaGuardia and was given clearance and a runway assignment.

By the time he was given the runway assignment at LaGuardia, Captain Sullenberger realized he would not be able to make the turn back due to the loss of thrust. He asked permission to enact an emergency landing at Teterboro Airport in New Jersey, across the Hudson River. The air traffic controllers contacted Teterboro Airport immediately and were given clearance. However, even in the few seconds that this took for them to do, Sullenberger announced, "We can't do it." and "We're gonna be in the Hudson."

What was clear at this point was that he intended to attempt a controlled ditching into the Hudson River. At approximately six minutes after take-off, Captain Sullenberger successfully piloted his aircraft, without power, into the Hudson River while traveling approximately one hundred and fifty miles per hour. All the passengers and crew were rescued successfully; and most with only minor injuries despite the extreme conditions under which Captain Sullenberger and his crew needed to act.

The entire crew of US Airways Flight 1549 of January 15, 2009 under the direction of Captain Sullenberger received the Master's Medal of the Guild of Air Pilots and Navigators, a highly regarded and distinguished award for aviators. The citation given with the award read: "This emergency ditching and evacuation, with the loss of no lives, is a heroic and unique aviation achievement."

In approximately six minutes, Captain Sullenberger and the entire crew were required to make numerous significant decisions to ensure the safety of their charges and produce the remarkable outcome that resulted. One of the unique statements made by Captain Sullenberger after the event was that he made the decision on where to ditch the aircraft based on his training. He chose a location where he could see several boats operating so as to maximize the chance of rescue.

Crisis Decision-Making

The example above of Captain Sullenberger's actions in regard to the successful controlled ditching of US Airways Flight 1549 is a brilliant example of crisis decision-making. According to one of the world's leading experts on crisis decision-making, Gary Klein, this kind of decision-making is dependent on the mental maps and models of the decision-maker to execute successfully.

In a situation such as this, there is no time for analysis or even prolonged consideration of options. Rather than seeking the best option, "any option which is good enough" will do. Fortunately for the passengers and crew of US Airways Flight 1549, Captain Sullenberger's experience and training enabled him, with the mental map and models he needed, to safely ditch the aircraft.

A significant amount of the research conducted on crisis decision-making, or as it is sometimes referred to as "naturalistic" decision-making, was conducted in relation to decision-makers who are responsible for making what amount to life and death decisions, such as those required by Captain Sullenberger to have been making in the example given above.

Typical contexts referred to by Gary Klein in his seminal book, "Sources of Power," included fire fighting, pre-natal intensive care units, operating rooms, and the like. In each of these contexts the life and death decisions that are being made are significantly dependent on the previous experience of the decision-maker in identical or similar situations, or from training in simulations that match the conditions in which the immediate decision is being made.

While dramatic, this kind of decision-making seldom relates to the kind of decisions made in most business contexts and provides little value when trying to improve the decision-making skills of leaders in business. Yet there is something of enormous value to be learned from understanding the structure of "Sully's" extraordinary decision-making prowess under significant stress.

Analytical Decision-Making

The most common type of decision-making referred to in business, and taught to business leaders is known as "analytical decision-making."

This kind of decision-making is dependent on the analysis of pre-existing data, often with the help of analytical tools for performing "What-If?" scenario building. With the advent of sophisticated computer programs to run these scenarios this kind of decision-making has become the rage.

The often-flawed presumption of analytical decision-making is that a previous trend will shed predictive light on future scenarios. Yet, becoming overly dependent on this kind of thinking about decision-making can lead to significant disasters, like those that led up to the worldwide economic crash of 2008/2009.

Despite significant evidence that "previous results are no guarantee of future performance" sophisticated analysis of trends in the financial marketplace were carried out by the world's leading experts based almost exclusively on past trends, who were subsequently uniformly caught unaware when the system imploded. These types of examples are just as plentiful in the corridors and boardrooms of small and large businesses of every size, in every sector, and in every location you might care to look.

However, when most business leaders refer to decision-making, what they are actually talking about is information-driven analysis. The most significant challenge to analytical decision-making is that it is dependent on having all the requisite data necessary to building accurate scenarios, or much worse, the 'presumption' that all the requisite data necessary is present.

So, what does this mean for business leaders seeking a means to improve their own decision-making?

Strategic Decision-Making

First, it is essential that we agree that by "business leader" we are referring to an individual who is responsible for defining and executing organizational strategy, whether we are looking at a local small business owner or the CEO of a global conglomerate. In their respective organizations, these folks are the senior business leaders.

The type of decision-making that is most relevant to senior business leaders is strategic decision-making. This kind of decision-making is related to implementing the strategy of the organization, regardless of whether or not the leader in question is a solo practitioner or a leader in a large multi-national with tens of thousands of employees.

Strategic decision-making has two essential elements at its core:

A - Intentionality

-and-

B - Consequences

Taken in sequence, these two elements are the primary tools of effective decision-making for senior business leaders who must make decisions that impact both the immediate and long-term success of the organization.

Intentionality as a Strategic Advantage

Intentionality is an expression of the idea of directionality in business - where the organization is going, how it is going to get there and most importantly, why is that the intention of the business.

Much of the time only a limited amount of the data they would like to have access to is available to most senior business leaders. This is just the simple reality of operating in a complex system. Regardless of whether the complex system is the community surrounding and supporting a small local retailer, or the complex web involving supply-chains and markets spanning the globe. Yet despite the limitations imposed by the inability to access all the data that they would like to have, business leaders are called upon daily to make decisions regarding the creation and implementation of organizational strategy.

So it would be fair to say that business leaders are often making decisions in a vacuum regarding the data they would like to have but do not. Two of the most common examples of this are:

Decisions in relation to what the competition is doing (or about to do)

-and-

Decisions about people within their own organization

While both examples refer to critical issues for business leaders, the first is perhaps more obvious in regard to the lack of data that is available. In the example of decisions about people in the organization, what is elusively obvious, is how much information about the individuals in the organization remains beyond the reach or awareness of the organization - or its leaders. Everyone associated with the business has a life that extends beyond the business which is constantly in play with regard to how they interact with and within that business. Yet most of this information about people in the organization is simply not accessible and cannot be included in the critical decisions concerning them as they relate to the business.

However, the business leader who can and does consider both what they know and what they don't know - without being hampered or bound by either - has a unique advantage over their contemporaries who can't and/or don't do the same. This is largely a question of intentionality, or keeping the business aimed in the right direction on a moment-to-moment basis without losing track of the long-term outcomes, or losing sight of the bigger picture.

Consequences and Decision-Making for Business Leaders

There are always two kinds of consequences that are associated with any decision. These are the positive and/or negative consequences. It is very likely that both types of consequences will be present. This brings us to a critical definition in our discussion of decision-making for business leaders, the definition of high quality decisions.

High quality decisions are those that maximize positive consequences, while simultaneously minimizing negative consequences.

This is a critical definition in an uncertain environment. It can be generally assumed that every decision brings with it both positive and negative consequences of some kind. Yet too often the focus overly emphasizes one type of consequence to the detriment of the overall outcome.

One result of the tendency to look more closely at the positive consequences than the negative consequences is that the organization gets caught by surprise and without the necessary resources to regroup and emerge from a situation that has gone bad successfully. A prime example of this would be the 2009 bailout of some the largest U.S. banks made necessary by missing the potential negative consequences of the combination of sub-prime lending and a precipitous drop in real-estate values. It could be argued that this caused the collapse of CountryWide, one of the largest mortgage institutions operating prior to the sub-prime bailout.

On the other hand, looking too closely at the negative consequences can cause equally disastrous outcomes due to the decision-making paralysis that is likely to ensue. What is required is a reasonable balance between the two forces contained in the positive and negative so that the path most likely to lead to the intended outcome is chosen.

The most critical task of any senior business leader is making the best decision possible with the limited data available in any and every given situation.

Almost always, the organization looks to the senior business leader to provide the way and point out the path. For the solo business owner there is no one but themselves to whom they can turn to point out the best way.

Bringing It All Together ... Incorporating the Full 'Scope of Decision'

Ultimately what saved the day on January 15, 2009 was the highly effective combination of intuition, training and experience that Captain Sullenberger possessed as the leader in that situation. In addition, his ability to translate that powerful combination into a series of decisions with the requisite necessary action made all the difference and acting with great intentionality, i.e., keeping the primary outcome of the safety of his passengers first and foremost. In doing this, he began by recognizing, accepting and incorporating the emerging data inherent in the situation to maximize the positive consequences, while simultaneously minimizing the negative consequences.

Deciding and acting in relation to the total data present in the system, and relating it to the immediate and the long-term consequences, is taking into account the full *Scope of Decision*. This is the essence of truly effective decision-making.

Becoming an effective decision-maker as a business leader requires moving beyond either crisis decision-making or analytical decision-making and begin using a strategic decision-making model. Strategic decision-making not only generates the strongest long-term results but it also extends the positive consequences further out into the organization, and even potentially beyond it.

Ray Anderson, CEO of Interface Carpet, is a great example of a leader using strategic decision-making to take into account the full *Scope of Decision* in the larger business system. He did this when he put his company on course to what he called "Mission Zero," i.e., eliminating any negative impact on the environment. Ray Anderson chose this course well before it became trendy for corporations to become *green*. He went beyond the accepted data and trusted well-honed business intuition, along with his substantial experience as an entrepreneur and business leader.

In the case of Interface Carpet, as a result of Ray Anderson's strategic decision-making, the organization built the institutional memory necessary to make these decisions. The outcome of the path that Ray Anderson set included greater public awareness and support of the brand, as well as significant savings and increased profitability.

Getting It (Mostly) Right ... Or the Art of Improving Along the Way

The task of making critical business decisions, like that of putting Interface Carpet on the path to "Mission Zero," is not unlike the decision-making that fell on the shoulders of Captain Sullenberger on January 15, 2009. The "crew" will be looking to the leader and the "life and death" of the business may well rest on the decisions that the leader makes ... or not.

The larger challenge is also not unlike the one that faced "Sully" on that fateful day, i.e., working with limited data, limited options and the need to act despite what is not known before taking action.

The primary difference however, is not tactical, i.e., about what to do or how to be doing it in the moment, but rather strategic and one of scale and scope. A business leader seldom has just seconds to decide and act. Instead the role of the business leader is to set the outcome for the organization based on reflection and a consideration of what is most desired; and then to set the direction ... NOT the absolute path or process to be followed indefinitely.

> *Literally, the strategic business leader must become comfortable and at ease in "not knowing" - and become open to a process of continuous learning, updating and adapting based on the emergent data flow in the system in which they are operating and making decisions.*

Rather than trying to get the next dozen decisions right before beginning to act, it would be better for the strategic business leader to set the strategy, take action, and learn to listen for the feedback coming from the system. In other words, the strategic business leader in making high-quality decisions acts with the long-view in mind, while only absolutely committing to the next single step to be taken.

In their continuous pursuit of achieving the goals Ray Anderson set for Interface Carpet, both he and the organization put in place a process for continually updating the system based on the feedback created by the actions taken. This new and emergent data is then fed back into the decision-making process, allowing for creativity and adaptability in regard to the actions that follow from the decisions previously made and implemented. Operating in this way requires a complete acceptance and realization of what you don't know as you continue moving the process forward.

This is a very challenging and difficult concept for most business leaders to learn. Maybe the single most challenging aspect for most business leaders is giving up the idea that they are "supposed to know the answers" before acting. This would go a long way in explaining why there is such a prevalence of analytical decision-making in business. If nothing else, analytical decision-making creates the illusion that what needs to be known to make high-quality decisions is present and has been considered. Rather than accept the reality that a decision is required when there is less than adequate data to make it, most business leaders will fall back on the faulty premise that they can count on their analytical tools to make their decisions for them.

Learning to let go of analysis as the basis for decision-making frequently comes with the heavy cost of significant trial and error. It also comes with the associated failures that accompany that particular learning strategy. Yet, there are other ways to significantly lessen costly trial and error, like bringing on highly seasoned professionals in various capacities. They will mentor the leader through this challenging learning process to build the innate capacity and the associated institutional memory that comes with it.

While the challenge of learning what may be a new and unfamiliar decision-making strategy may seem fraught with danger; the rewards significantly outweigh the risk in the longer term, and the wise business leader does not have to go it alone.

At the end of the day, the business leader who makes the investment to develop the skills of strategic decision-making will be richly rewarded for his efforts. Hopefully, before the day when they have to confront the equivalent of "Sully's" controlled ditching of US Airways Flight 1549 in the Hudson River, they will have made the investment in themselves to be ready to act with the same kind of calm élan and aplomb.

Joseph Riggio, Ph.D. is the founder of the JS Riggio Institute for Leadership Transformation and the president of the consulting firm, Joseph Riggio International. He works globally as a trusted adviser and mentor to senior executives in Fortune 500 companies, entrepreneurs, business owners and professionals. Dr. Riggio specializes in strategic decision-making for leaders and learning design for leadership development and his professional work is frequently referenced. Joseph is also the author of the book Towards A Theory of Transpersonal Decision-Making in Human Systems *and a keynote speaker. You can find out more about Dr. Riggio on-line at: http://www.jsri.com.*

6 | Leadership

Leadership Keys That Drive Business

By Harlan Goerger

I t's an all too familiar site – one day the "Open" sign is hanging brightly on the front door then, before you know it, a "Closed" sign is dangling outside. You know the owner, Aaron, a trusted and well respected business owner. What happened ... everyone liked him and it seemed like his business was flourishing?

What seemed like a viable business with potential became casualty to internal faltering. Upon further investigation ... the source of failure was lack of effective leadership! There were problems stemming from poor leadership, which included: cash flow mismanagement, employee problems, over worked owners and poor marketing.

Successful leaders use the following keys for long-term business success:

Key 1: VISION

Aaron's dream came true—he jumped in with two feet and opened a business. Technically competent in the video industry, he could make almost anything work when it came to cameras or video production.

Even though Aaron had a business idea and was an expert in his industry, he lacked a clear and descriptive vision. His employees didn't understand the direction or vision of the business and neither did his customers.

A clear and strong vision of your business is so important – it becomes the star, the goal, the direction of the business. How can a successful business owner lead if he or she has no direction? The vision of your business should be very simple, clear and meaningful so that every employee and even your customers can understand it.

A word of caution – many business owners create insightful documents called "Vision" and "Mission" statements complete with elaborate words, acceptable axioms and company values. Problems arise because no one understands the meaning, the communication falls short, and no one cares about it or uses it. What value is this other than a plaque on the wall for visitors to read?

Here's an easy way to know if your vision hits the mark. Simply ask, "When you think of your company, what words come to mind?"

For example, a client in the Agricultural Manufacturing field answered, "A team of people, working together to build the best dryers there are."

"That's a great Vision! Are you communicating that throughout the company?" I asked.

Well … they are now! Here's a quick diagnosis of why something this simple works:

When a team of people work together (using values, teamwork, communication, collaboration) they are focused on continuous product improvement, on quality assurance and on customer relations, to become world class. Is more needed to be effective?

Absolutely, as a business leader, your vision must be conveyed to your employees through company communications such as in formal meetings, casual conversations, and daily interaction. Now, if there is a decision needed or action to be taken, an employee would know exactly what to do and how it would affect the business and leadership.

Key Vision Points:

1. Be clear, vivid, and meaningful so that everyone understands your vision.

2. Communicate the vision every day.

3. Answer these questions...

   a. Who are you?

   b. Who is the company?

   c. What are the key values that guide you?

   d. What culture do you want to build?

Your answers to the above questions will help you formulate your vision statement which will become a cornerstone for successful leadership.

Key 2: Communications

Investigation into Aaron's business included an analysis of his communication dynamics. Aaron tended to "tell" everyone what he wanted and then go about his business. To get a clearer picture of communication effectiveness, several questions had to be asked.

"Aaron, when you opened this business, how did your thinking evolve from being an employee to now being a business owner?"

Aaron replied, "Dramatically, I had so many more things to think about and do. I had to know everything about everything and continually be looking ahead at every turn. It wasn't just about getting the job done anymore."

"And how does your thinking as a business owner differ from your employees' thinking about this business?" I asked.

"They just didn't seem to understand the importance of things or getting tasks done right and on time. It seems like I had to push people all the time!" responded Aaron.

Aaron was missing a key point about leadership. Communication is not about "telling" others what you want. It's about having "meaningful conversations." The word "conversation" infers information flows both ways ... not just from leadership down to employees.

Successful leaders listen more than they talk; because true motivation and commitment comes from within others, not just the leader. This requires leaders to stop, listen, and understand those whom they are leading.

To help you understand the fine points of communication, here is a quick overview of different communication styles according to the DISC Behavioral Styles Model:

<u>D</u> is a very dominant style with quick decisions and actions. Their motivations are outcomes and results.

<u>I</u> is very influential, needs people around, and is very persuasive. They are motivated by relationships and connections to others.

<u>S</u> is a steady and supportive type who gets it done right. This type needs lots of trust and no change, and is motivated by helping others and looking out for others.

<u>C</u> is very analytically competent and loves numbers and research. Their motivation is through accuracy and avoiding errors.

Four different behavioral styles view the world differently and are motivated differently. Imagine trying to communicate and motivate these four types the same way. What challenges or results might this create?

To make things more interesting, let's add elements such as: personal values, beliefs, cultural and religious backgrounds. Can a leader afford not to understand where people's views come from?

Aaron now takes a different approach to communication, this time with a very clear, solid and understandable vision. He has "meaningful conversations" where he asks meaningful questions about vision, values and motivations. He discovers how others understand the vision and the business. He sees their views and motivations, helps them fit these into his vision and his team. Aaron has these "meaningful conversations" regularly; most staff meetings become this type of conversation. There is feedback from the employees because leadership is truly listening and guiding, not simply telling and demanding. How do you see this changing his business outcomes? Will this have employees thinking and acting like the owner? Probably not, they are still employees; but they will have clear direction and understanding of your business and know they are assets to be valued.

Another critical aspect of communication in leadership is the "numbers." The vision gives people direction, but they also need measurements in their progress towards expectations.

Aaron felt he needed to keep everything to himself, including how well the business was doing. When things were going poorly, he feared the employees would talk and probably leave if told the real picture. The closing came as a complete surprise to everyone; they thought things were great.

When asked, the employees indicated they would have dug in and worked harder if they knew the business was suffering. They had ideas of how the business could have improved, but there was no "meaningful conversations" so the ideas were never communicated.

Should leaders give everyone the Profit and Loss statements? No, but there are six important numbers that make a difference and indicate how the business is doing. These numbers should be part of those "meaningful conversations" meetings. These numbers are different for each business, but they are crucial in communicating the health of the business, give employees an idea of how they are doing personally, and spur new ideas. These should be continually communicated in a way that assures each employee understands the meaning and potential outcomes from these numbers. Here is the reality about people; give them part of the picture and they will creatively fill in the gaps with their own enlarged and erroneous information. Now you have misinformation as truth and rumors fly.

By consistently having "meaningful conversations" about the vision, six important numbers and the understanding of the business; a leader creates a culture that energizes people and moves the organization forward.

Key Communications Points:

1. "Listen" more than "tell."

2. Use "meaningful conversations" to convey the business vision.

3. Understand DISC Behavioral styles, motivations, beliefs and values to gain true commitment.

4. Communicate the vision continually and consistently, and ask for feedback.

Key 3: Leadership by Example

In discussions with Aaron he said, "I never asked someone to do what I haven't done and I got right in there with them and did it." These were huge red flags in terms of leadership capability and created leadership downfall.

Aaron was a great technician and understood the video technical side. As a business owner, he also dealt with personnel issues, payroll, accounting, taxes, promotion, advertising, building maintenance, etc. He hated it and did not understand it; yet because of mistrust issues, he did it himself. Invoices were always late, payroll was rushed and his collections and cash flow were in disarray. Should Aaron have led by example by doing everything himself? Managers, executives and owners do this because they erroneously feel they need to "Lead by Example."

Called in to solve a problem, Aaron typically pushed the others aside and did it himself. He was the most competent and could do it timely and efficiently. But, here is what leadership should be doing. In Aaron's new approach to leadership, he stops, questions what's happening and asks himself why. He asks the employees to do certain tasks based on their skills and then observes as they take care of the issue. This is called "coaching" which builds others' abilities to perform successfully.

Everyone has strengths and capabilities. The leadership role is to use each person's strengths to their greatest advantage of the organization in alignment with the vision. Aaron, trying to do everything himself, ended up killing his business and he was doing things he was not good at nor understood. Perhaps as a business leader, you feel putting in 80-90 hour work weeks are a requirement for a successful business... but it's not. Aaron admitted he should have outsourced many tasks and concentrated on steering the business. Coaching his people was one of his most important tasks as a leader, yet he invested no time in coaching. Mistakenly he believed there were more important things to do.

Business leaders should create the matrix below to align tasks with the correct abilities and strengths of the team.

1. List every task and action that is required to run the business day to day in one column.

2. List the skills and abilities needed for each task in the next column.

3. List the leader's true skills and abilities where they matched in the third column.

4. Where leader's skills did not match up, find someone with matching skills to do it.

5. Mark the most important tasks based on the vision, limited to six.

6. Mark where the leader's strengths match with one or all of the six tasks.

7. If several of the six tasks do not match the leader's skills, then learn or develop those skills.

Aaron can focus on the six most important aspects of his business while coaching others and outsourcing those areas that are not his strengths. This gives him time to monitor all the areas he has delegated so he is still in contact and control.

Six areas of focus is a maximum most people can psychologically handle at one time. Oftentimes, executives narrow the list to three tasks to categorize. This results in more focus, less stress, and higher productivity.

In Aaron's new approach to his business, he creates the three-six key tasks to focus his vision and categorizes the most important actions needed in each area. This helps him guide his employees on the most important aspects needing attention which ultimately leads to increased productivity.

With his new processes in place, Aaron is called into action doing something he probably shouldn't. But, once the short crisis pasts, he has time and resources to examine the how and why, thus eliminates the problem the correct way.

Key Leadership Points:

1. Know your strengths and the strengths of your employees; and focus them in the right areas for the right reasons.

2. Focus on the three to six most critical aspects of your business. Set an example of openness and responsibility throughout your company.

3. Outsource and coach others for the tasks you shouldn't be doing.

Key 4: Power of Consistency

The way to successfully "lead by example" is through consistency! When a leader takes a stand or consistently performs or behaves in a given way, others trust him/her. People resist change and want consistency and predictability in their lives. Aaron would say, "Do it this way" and then did the task another way. This confused people and generated mistrust among his employees.

This also occurs when treating internal employees by different standards than customers or vendors. Aaron was great with customers, handling complaints with a pleasant smile, only to turn on employees for the slightest of errors. This inconsistent treatment of people leads to mistrust and feelings of ingratitude.

When people are not sure of expectations, it generates fear in various forms. "Is the boss in a good or bad mood today?" This conversation starter among employees is a red flag. It means leadership is inconsistent with attitude and behavior, leading to speculation of the problem. Your employees, not understanding you, will fill in the gaps and rumors will spread creating more mistrust and fear. You now have created a culture that does not communicate or trust leadership.

Business leaders, such as Aaron, are also challenged in responsibility and accountability. A problem arose in Aaron's business and a witch-hunt followed by tracking a scapegoat to pin it on. Even if it was Aaron's fault, it confused the employees. Owners are responsible for everything that happens, good or bad. By consistently demonstrating this accountability, leadership builds trust and credibility internally and externally.

Consistency also applies to important activities. If the staff meeting with "meaningful conversations" is continually postponed, it then becomes unimportant. If it were important, it would be consistently the same time. If appraisals are delayed and changed, what happens to appraisal value in the employee's eyes?

To "lead by example" the correct way, consistency is the way to do it – build trust, respect and loyalty from both employees and customers.

Key Consistency Points:

1. Take responsibility and accountability – for yourself first.
2. Have consistent activities and / or actions for your team.
3. Consistent actions reduce fear in others and create positive expectations, so be consistent in personal actions, thinking and communication.

Key 5: Decisions & Directions

In examining Aaron's situation, the decision making process was lacking. In business, decisions are made daily, some with little information and significant impact.

Aaron's decision making inconsistencies were weakening his leadership abilities. Employees wanted firm decisions in a timely manner but it rarely occurred. He would ask opinions and gather information when making decisions, but this delayed him even more.

The bottom-line on decisions; someone has to be accountable for every decision in business, be it the owner or the employee. Every group looks to those that make decisions as their leader and expects them to hold to those decisions. Someone may disagree with a given choice, but allowing them to participate and be heard is generally enough. When the leader says, "This is the decision," the group goes along with it even if they do not agree. Remember, it is your business, so make the decisions accordingly.

The vision should direct the thinking. You should be able to answer the following questions when making decisions: Do your decisions fit the company vision? In communications and "meaningful conversations" — does it make sense to the team and you? Does it fit with your three major areas of focus and should it be your decision? If you answered yes to all, then go ahead.

If new information arises, is it ok to change the decision? Yes, just be sure to communicate this new information so others understand the reason for the change.

Someone has to carry out the associated tasks. The art of delegation is chapters unto itself; thus, some brief key points to keep in mind:

1. When assigning a task, have specific outcomes that align with the vision. Communicate expectations; ask for feedback and verification for understanding. Short cut this and you will have issues.

2. Ask the employee their view of the task and how they would tackle it. Even if you have a specific procedure, this dialog helps them buy in and verifies their understanding of outcomes.

3. Have a specific conversation about expectations and measurements. The clearer these are the more self-directed people will be. If this step does not exist, how will you hold anyone accountable? Keep it as simple and direct as possible, the idea of three key focus points works here.

4. Keep consistent communications going and monitor the progress. Coach the employees as needed to help them meet the marks.

5. When the task is successfully completed, give feedback as to

what they did right. Ask what they might do differently and how the task could improve. This builds for future projects and allows employees to expand their thinking.

Remember — critical points in decisions and directions — have the right person in place for the right reasons.

Key Decision Points:

1. Leaders are accountable for decisions, make them and move on; if changed, communicate the why.

2. Directions need to align with the vision, be specific and verify with feedback.

3. Reward and reevaluate.

Summary

The 5 key components detailed in this chapter are essential to every successful business leader.

1. Vision needs to be clear, communicated and understandable as this drives all leadership thinking and actions.

2. "Meaningful Conversations" motivate, connect and inspire.

3. Focus on three key tasks, delegate the rest.

4. Consistency drives trust and productivity.

5. Make decisions and move on while directing others with specifics, measurements and expectations.

Harlan Goerger is author of The Selling Gap, Selling Strategies for the 21st Century. *With 30 years in the field consulting and training leaders in all types and sizes of business, Harlan has discovered what works and what does not. One difference that Harlan brings to his clients is the application of Ethical Persuasion Science to Leadership and Sales. He is President of H. Goerger & Associates, Inc. in Fargo, North Dakota and works with business leaders to improve the performance of their teams, key people and sales forces. He can be contacted at HHG@HGoergerAssoc.com www.HGoergerAssoc.com www.TheSellingGap.com www.AskHG.com*

7 | Hiring Sales People

A Group Approach to Hiring Sales Stars

By Danita Bye

Smart business, at its core, is all about Return on Investment. So, it follows that smart business is smart asset acquisition and management. And a sales team that gets results is the most important asset for any company. Since nothing happens without a sale, recruitment and hiring a high-performance sales team should be at the top of a business leader's priority list.

Filling a sales position is frustrating and mistakes are costly. Business owners throw away thousands of dollars in recruiting and training underperforming salespeople, not to mention lost sales and customer defections. Some estimates place the cost of a bad hire at $100,000 to $250,000. Others warn that bad hires waste 100% to 265% the annual cost of the terminated salesperson. Worse, for senior-level salespeople, the figure can be much higher. In his book *Top Grading*, Dr. Bradford Smart notes that a hiring mistake can cost more than $800,000.

Sorting Out an Ideal Salesperson's DNA

Hiring a salesperson is different from hiring, say, an accountant. The reason is the DNA. No one is a born accountant, but strong salespeople have certain untrainable qualities built in. While I'm not saying a stellar salesperson does not require training and management, you cannot develop a star when the DNA is missing.

The combination of DNA that will make a star salesperson for your company will depend on your culture, customers, sales process, what you are selling, among other factors. That said, there are universals, including a strong sense of personal responsibility and a tenacious desire to succeed despite obstacles.

These traits and a few others make up what I call the "adversity response cluster" of high-performance sales DNA. Together, they are imperative for success in a job defined by adversity and must be present from the outset as I learned early in my career as owner/manager of a struggling medical device company.

At the start, we were virtually unknown. We had all the problems common to a young company and our prospects were not bright. However, we grew from $300,000 to a run rate of $20 million in revenues in just a few years. That would not have been possible if we had hired in the traditional way, a way that often misses key, inborn traits. But because we learned from the outset to find and hire those traits, especially an inbuilt tolerance for adversity, we did not waste time and money vainly hoping to train qualities that were not present in the first place.

Step One: Unravel Your Model Salesperson's DNA

According to a University of Michigan study, interviews lead to almost 90% of hiring decisions but are only 14% accurate in predicting success. Why? Using resumes and interviews to hire is a little like buying a suit off the rack – unless you are extremely lucky, it will never fit just right. That's why it is so important to learn exactly what you need and then buy a suit – a salesperson – with a custom fit.

It is a surprising and sad fact that too many business owners hire salespeople without really taking the time to analyze what the DNA of a great salesperson would look like in their industry and culture. But even if they know what DNA they need, can they find those genes with resumes and interviews? No, for (at least) two reasons:

1. The resume is what the candidate *wishes* his or her DNA was, not what it actually is.

2. Skills to be successful with a different industry, product, or culture mean little for success in your environment.

When hiring criteria is framed in general terms, as it is when relying on resumes and interviews alone, your odds of a good hire drop significantly. So, defining the specific sales DNA for your sales organization is a critical first step.

Defining the requirements of your ideal salesperson

The task of sequencing your ideal salesperson's DNA breaks down into four components:

1. Profile your market industry. How sophisticated are the clients you target? What are the technical requirements of the products/services you sell? How many competitors exist in your market, and how aggressive are they? How long is the sell cycle? How large is a typical order? For example, in my own medical device company, I needed salespeople who had the capacity to sell higher-end products – where we had stiff competition from entrenched market leaders – to audiologists and doctors. I looked for a unique DNA.

2. Define the daily requirements of the position. How much prospecting do you expect from your salesperson? How much travel is required? Will salespeople work on the phone, and do they present to groups? Is customer service a priority? Are there heavy documentation requirements? How sophisticated is your sales process?

3. Profile needed skills. Must salespeople be detail-oriented problem solvers? Will a focus on strategy or a talent for organization aid them? Do you expect a high level of technical knowledge, well-developed written communication skills, or presentation know-how?

4. Write a clearly defined job description. After determining key accountabilities and skills, rank them and weight them. Make sure that the job description clearly defines required skills, job responsibilities, and the metrics by which salespeople will be measured. This will be your starting point for Step 2.

    Note that the work you do in this step may not reflect your current staff requirements. In any case, focus on an ideal scenario for accomplishing your strategic growth objectives.

Step Two: Write and Place the Ad

With a clear job description in hand, you are ready to write the ad that causes the reader to self-qualify, to perk up and say, "That's me! They are looking for someone just like me!" or move on after saying, "I would never want a job like that." This type of ad quickly separates you from 95% of the other competitive ads; it jumps out at the candidate that has the DNA you need.

Because you have completed Step One, much of the work involved in writing the ad is done, but here are three rules to follow:

*   Do write a heading that makes readers want to find out more. Here, you are looking for a brief, interesting title which adequately describes the general scope of the job, does not prematurely disqualify readers, and aligns with a typical search engine query.

*   Do begin your ad with "must haves." Follow with "should haves," income requirements, company description, call to action, and contact information, in that order. For instance, when hiring my team, I listed the following "must haves": successful track record of prospecting and bringing in new clients in a competitive market.

*   Do not describe your company in great detail. Describe the candidate instead. Think of your ad as an ideal candidate-shaped hole into which readers can mentally fit themselves.

Once the ad is written, get it in front of as many potential candidates as possible. I strongly suggest using online search boards like Monster or CareerBuilder, which make it easy for candidates to search for and receive e-email alerts about positions that match their income and career criteria.

Step Three: Screen and Shortlist Candidates

Defining the DNA you need and writing a good ad will ensure some measure of self-qualification for the resumes you will receive, but in today's market you are likely to get 60 to 120! So, in this step, you will qualify them further – and get closer to finding your star salesperson – with as little effort as possible.

Using online tools saves time

Another reason I advise using online search boards like Monster or CareerBuilder is their time-saving automation features, particularly automated screening questionnaires that must be passed before a candidate can apply for a position. Even though your ad clearly states your criteria, some candidates will ignore them and send you their resume anyway. By including questions related to your key qualifications in these questionnaires, you can quickly eliminate over 50% of prospective candidates.

For example, your position might require 50% travel, a four-year science degree, 10 years of industry-specific experience, and three years earning over $100K. Though most unqualified candidates will not complete the application process, those who do apply generate flags for not meeting criteria. I typically ask about 10 questions, and following the online screen I'll typically wind up with 20 to 30 candidates that meet my criteria, which is great since I like smaller piles of paper.

Screening for DNA

At this stage of the process I recommend a detailed sales assessment customized to screen for position-critical DNA. This assessment has been validated to eliminate major hiring mistakes, and it will tell me if a candidate can and will sell in this specific setting. This assessment generates a report of each candidate tested, beginning with a *Hirable* or *Not Hirable* recommendation and continuing with a comprehensive roundup of the test data that forms the basis of that recommendation. Even better, it offers specific interview questions to further validate its findings.

By using an assessment tool, you will not only know that candidates meet your criteria, you will also know they can sell, all without even scanning a resume. Since this system is so focused and streamlined, you will also be able to shortlist qualified candidates in less time than simply reviewing dozens of resumes that likely contain inflated claims.

Once you are left with around 10 qualified candidates, thank those who do not fit your needs and move the rest on to the next stage, the phone screen.

Screening your candidates by phone

Before screening candidates by phone, create a short scorecard to rate them quickly and systematically. The important thing is to standardize the questions you will ask so that you can track phone screen responses in a reliable and repeatable way while saving time. Each telephone screen should take only 10 to 12 minutes.

Rate candidates on the following: warmth, the ability to ask good questions and their pacing on the phone screen, as well as their cultural fit, experience, and technical skills. MOST IMPORTANTLY, rate candidates highly for trying to close you on hiring them. In fact, do not further consider anyone who does not try to close, not for a sales position.

Following your phone screen, only three or four candidates should remain.

Step Four: Invite Your Top Candidates to Interview

In this step, you will find out how your three or four remaining candidates fit your specific requirements and culture. By follow-ing the procedures here, you will gain a detailed understanding of their selling skills, attitudes, and compatibility with your company and its goals.

To get started, you will need a process to guide you, keep you in control of the interview, and ensure that all candidates are asked the same questions. This is important because sometimes you will like someone with similar interests and forget to ask the tough questions. In that case, you'll wind up hiring a friend, not a top performer. And your bottom line will suffer the consequences of a mis-hire.

Drafting interview questions and creating the post-interview

Before conducting your first interview cycle, script some behav-ioral interview questions, questions that zero in on how to behave in critical selling situations, and create a post-interview scorecard that you will complete immediately after speaking with each can-didate. This scorecard will be similar to those used in the last step but geared specifically toward the questions you are asking in this interview.

Conducting and reviewing the first interview

This first interview builds on the insight you gain from your screen-ing and gives you an opportunity to observe composure, style, ma-turity, and resilience. It is not, however, a popularity contest, and you are not looking for the "nicest" one of the bunch. Focus instead of verifying a good fit with your organization and goals. As noted by Jacques Werth, President of High Probability Selling, only 3% of customers buy based on good rapport with their salespeople. The other 97% buy from salespeople who, while they may be nice, are closers.

After numerous mis-hires of my own, I learned the importance of watching the candidates' closing and objection-handling behav-ior as part of the interview. I learned that the type of closing behavior I needed is not, "What's the next step in your process?" To grow revenues, I needed salespeople who could consistently gain commitments on each interaction with my client. To succeed, they needed persistence.

How many people should conduct the interviews? I recommend a mix of interviewers, each with a different personality type, to give you a wider view of the candidates. By tripling the interviews, you will get points of comparison on your scorecards that can be invaluable for eliminating bias.

Immediately after each interview, while candidate responses and your impressions are still fresh in your mind, complete your post-interview scorecard. With scorecards in hand, plus the data from your screen, select your two best candidates, who then move on to Step Five.

Step Five: Final Interview with Your Top Two Candidates

Step Five is all about eliminating surprises. In my days as a sales manager and owner, I hated surprises. I still do. In particular, I really disliked learning post-hire that I had made a mistake and was throwing my hard-earned profits right out the window.

To avoid that, you are going to take a hard look at your remaining candidates with a second set of assessments and a second interview. This step gets much more specific about the responsibilities of the position and your expectations; giving you more insight into what motivates your top two candidates and whether they are going to fit your organizational culture and management style.

I cannot stress enough how important it is that your new hire fit with your management style. One time, for example, I hired a great salesperson who tested well on talents and skills. He had the background I was looking for and interviewed like a champ. But he had low self-start and self-management capabilities, and this meant that he cornered me two or three times each day, asking me to figure things out for him – things that he should have been able to figure out on his own.

After this final round, you should have a good idea which of your two remaining candidates is the one for you. But talk to them both anyway, if only to ask two questions: "Has anything changed since our previous interview?" and "If we offer you the position, would there be anything to keep you from accepting?" Both of these questions uncover objections and minimize negotiation during the final stage.

Step Six: Hire and Fast Track

Once you have reached consensus on who is going to be the next star in your sales constellation, offer the position using an official letter. Be sure to congratulate and tell them how excited you are to have them on the team. Do not forget the additional paperwork, i.e., non-competes or background checks.

Start your new hire on the road to success with a 30-60-90 day fast-tracking plan.

When clients ask me what is the second most important step in this process after Step One, I invariably reply, "Step Six." The first 90 days will be make-or-break for your new hire. Even though you have done your best to find a star salesperson from the beginning, you will need 30-60-90-day fast-tracking and personal development plans, for a couple of reasons: First, if you did make a mistake, you will want to find out and act quickly. I often find that business owners wait one to two years "hoping" that they'll succeed. If you do not see the behavior and results during your fast-tracking period, it probably will not happen in one or two years. In other words, "Hire slowly, fire quickly." Second, without focus from the beginning, even a good sales rep will perform poorly. Third, the farther your salesperson is off track, the more effort it will take to correct his or her path.

Your personal development plan must address expected technical knowledge, sales skills, and activity levels. Also make sure you have a plan to develop identified weaknesses and capitalize on core strengths, including specific, measurable results and timelines to track progress.

This step is often overlooked, but if you do not define a clear track your new hire can run on, all your work to this point might be wasted. Not only do fast-tracking and personal development plans get the employee up to speed and producing quickly, they provide very clear direction on expectations during this critical adjustment phase.

Finally, Give Yourself a Pat on the Back

Congratulations! By following a process that puts objective assessment ahead of resumes and interviews that provide, at best, only an incomplete picture, you have saved time and hundreds of thousands of dollars in wasted costs. But more importantly, you will experience a rewarding Return on Investment and you have done the footwork to put your company on the success track for the long term.

Nationally recognized sales management expert, **Danita Bye***, is an acclaimed speaker, author and advisor who is valued for her expertise in propelling sales teams to reach ever-greater levels of success. As a recruiting expert, she assists in the hiring of over 1000 professional sales people each year, ensuring that new hires have the DNA to get results and meet her client's needs. "Hiring Smart" is a key growth strategy for her clients that yield impressive improvements in close rates, revenue growth and increased margins. Bull or bear, bust or boom, recession or recovery, Danita Bye will get the sales results needed.*

8 | Sales Compensation Plan Design

Compensate to Motivate Your Sales Team

By Lee B. Salz

O ne of the most critical decisions a small business owner makes is how to compensate their sales people. Unfortunately, many look at sales compensation from a single vantage point. *How much do we want our sellers to earn if they achieve quota?* While earnings are an important and relevant question, it is not the only consideration when designing an effective sales compensation plan.

What many business owners forget is that a sales compensation plan doubles as a job description which can be a blessing or a curse depending upon how it is structured. You can yell, scream, rant, and rave, but those outbursts won't affect sales behavior with the same level of impact as the message communicated by your compensation plan. As one executive shared after going through the aforementioned exercise, "We want our sales people to focus on selling our new product to existing clients. Yet, we are compensating the sales people in a way that they are financially better-off pursuing new clients." After a short pause – the light bulb went on...he got it!

There are many different drivers that can be used to trigger sales compensation beyond salary... revenue, gross margin, quota attainment, EBITDA, etc. Regardless of which driver(s) you select, there is a three-prong model that should be applied to any plan you develop ... *The Sales Compensation Equilateral Triangle™* (SCET™) model. As you know, the equilateral triangle is comprised of three equal sides. In the SCET™ model, the three sides represent three business entities: sales people, clients, and the company.

The equilateral triangle serves as the perfect model when designing sales compensation because it ensures none of the three entities are over or under recognized by the plan. If any side of the triangle is out of proportion, it results in the law of unintended consequences. Things happen to your business that are not intended, but are consistent with the message communicated by the plan. Here are some examples of compensation plans gone awry.

SCET™ Case Study: Health Club Chain

A health club chain offered a discounted membership program to businesses. Their clubs had two types of sales people -- membership and corporate. The membership sales people generated leads for the corporate sales people. The corporate sales people followed up on the leads and called the prospects offering a 20% membership discount for their employees ... if they would agree to promote the offer within their businesses.

In contrast to the SCET™ model, this program was a colossal failure. The company paid full commissions to both the membership and corporate sales people on 20% discounted memberships. Needless to say, the sales people were ecstatic and invested countless hours pushing this program instead of the other programs offered by the company *(the ones the company wanted them to sell)*.

The other two entities were much less satisfied with this offer. The company, because the memberships were heavily discounted and paid double commissions (not only to the sales people, but to their managers as well), came to realize that they had a near non-existent margin from this campaign. They also found that their corporate sales team dedicated all of their selling time to this program instead of other programs that produced a higher margin, but paid lower commission rates to the sales people.

When looking at the third side of the equilateral triangle, the clients, they saw no value in the program. The companies simply posted a flyer on a bulletin board and saw no tangible benefits. Further, when employees who joined the health club through this program were interviewed, most said that they were already planning to join at list price.

Thus, this compensation program failed two sides of the SCET™ model. Only the sales people won here.

SCET™ Case Study: Human Resources Outsourcing (HRO) Service Provider

A firm offering outsourced human resources services structured their compensation plan to pay commissions to their sellers at the highest percentage for the first 18-months following the signing of a new client contract. After that initial period, the commission rate dropped to a fraction of a percentage. At first glance, there didn't appear to be an issue with this compensation strategy, but there were major design flaws.

First, the 18-month clock never restarted for a client. This meant that if a sales person expanded the size of the account, they only received the commission rate commensurate with the moment in time of the client lifecycle. For example, if the sales person grew the account in month 19, the commission they were paid wasn't enough to buy a Starbuck's cup of coffee due to the drop in compensation level. The plan directed the sales people to sell whatever they could in the first 18-months of the contract and not to bother with up-selling or cross-selling as the additional compensation did not justify the work. The sales people did not like this plan at all because they felt the company received the growth benefits, but they didn't share in the success.

The clients suffered as a result of this compensation strategy as well. Since the commission rate for their sales person dropped after month 18, so did the level of sales person attentiveness to their account. The plan unintentionally directed that to happen. What made this an issue was that the sales people were expected to, not only sell services to the account, but provide client support as well. Why would sales people invest their time in account management when there were more financially beneficial activities for them to pursue? And, the sales people didn't.

The company wasn't happy with the results of the sales compensation plan either. The leadership team came to realize that their sales people were not focused on conquering accounts. The sales people made the initial sale and moved on to the next opportunity. The sales people weren't interested in expanding each account which meant missed revenue opportunities for the company. They were also losing many of their clients after 18 months as the attentiveness of the sales people waned.

Unlike in the health club example where the sales people were happy with the plan, but the clients and company were not, no one was happy with this plan. After two painful years, this sales compensation plan was scrapped in favor of one that met the criteria of the SCET™ model.

Designing the Plan

Management teams sit in board rooms with strategic plans of grandeur, but the plans collapse when they don't design the right sales compensation plan to drive the desired results. It is a very simple equation. Sales people invest their time on activities that affect their compensation. It's naïve to think that sales people will actively and consistently perform activities that are not in their financial best interests.

When structuring sales compensation plans, the starting point is to identify the goals of the company as they relate to the sales organization. Working backwards, the goals for the company drive the sales compensation plan and must be directly aligned. The sales people should be able to easily understand the message the plan communicates so they direct their activities accordingly.

If the corporate goal is to gain adoption of a new product in the marketplace, the plan should reward sales people for accomplishing this feat.

If the corporate goal is to increase revenue with the current clientele, the plan should reward for that.

If the corporate goal is to sell the highest margin products, the plan should pay at the top level for those achievements.

Further complicating matters, there are instances when sales people are compensated for delivering a certain set of results while their managers are compensated on a different set. Thus, the sales managers are driving their team to do what pads their wallet, but not what rewards their sales team.

For example, if the sales team is heavily compensated for generating new accounts, but the manager is handsomely rewarded for positioning a new product with existing clients – trouble is brewing! The incongruence of these plans can paralyze your entire sales organization. What happens when compensation between managers and their sales teams is not aligned? Try pushing a boulder up a hill. It's not going anywhere and neither is the top-line of your business.

This doesn't mean that sales managers and sales people need to be rewarded the same amount or even the same way. However, what cannot happen is for the two plans to be in conflict with one another.

Win, Lose, or DRAW!

In some complex sales environments (those with lengthy buying cycles), the standard salary and commission model does not create enough of a framework to ensure that the sales team performs the right activities every day. A sale won today does not mean that the sales person performed the right activities today, or even recently. If it takes a year to win an account, you know that your sales person did something right a year ago, but not necessarily yesterday or today.

In that example, the commission payment isn't necessarily reinforcing the desired behavior. There is an old sales expression, "You're only as good as your last sale." That expression is short-sighted for the small business owner. It leads to a pipeline that resembles an EKG report with huge peaks and valleys. A more effective mantra is "You're only as good as your <u>next sale</u>." Unlike the other expression, this one keeps the focus on, not only winning business today, but building a solid sales pipeline for tomorrow.

Another challenge for small business owners is recruiting strong sales talent when it takes a long time to earn commissions. Few strong sellers are willing to take a financial step backwards with the hopes of a future income boom. The kneejerk reaction of many small business owners is to provide a draw (*an advance payment of commissions*) to close the earnings gap. Nothing good comes from draws.

There are two types of draws: *recoverable* and *non-recoverable*. The recoverable draw is a loan against the sales people's future commissions. This type of draw, almost always, puts sales people under a financial strain. They wake up each morning knowing they owe the company money. No one enjoys the feeling of debt. It certainly doesn't build corporate loyalty.

The non-recoverable draw is money, free and clear, to the sales person for some duration of time. Often times, this type of draw creates an earnings cliff. Let's say that the non-recoverable draw is provided for three months at $2,000 per month. In the fourth month, the sales people probably experience a significant fall-off in their earnings. In addition, the company does not get any return on these dollars. There are no activity requirements or performance measures required to earn the dollars. It gives new definition to corporate waste.

How do you structure the sales compensation plan to bridge the earnings gap when recruiting new sales people and keep your existing team focused on performing the right activities at the desired frequency levels?

A Unique Sales Compensation Strategy

The challenge of motivating sales people and bridging the sales earnings gap can be addressed with a creative, non-traditional compensation approach. In the 1980s and 1990s, the big buzz term was MBO (Management by Objective). Business people were provided with a series of objectives and, following a performance review, were compensated for achievement. What if the MBO concept was applied to sales compensation? What if you created a *Sales Behavioral Objective*™ program (**SBO**™)?

This is not an additional sales expense, but rather a reallocation of a portion of the dollars paid to your sales people. A percentage of the dollars normally budgeted for commissions are allocated for an SBO bonus program.

Consider this. A company has a typical buying process that is six months long. They pay a sales person a base salary of $60,000. At 100% achievement of the plan, the sales person earns $90,000 ($30,000 over their base salary). However, no commissions are earned in his first six months of employment due to the length of the buying cycle. The company, as a strategy to drive specific sales behaviors and attract strong sales talent, budgets $15,000 of the $30,000 commission budget for the SBO bonus. The sales person becomes eligible to earn a $3,750 SBO bonus each quarter during their first year with the company.

When designing the SBO program, start with the new hire sales person and build the program expectations based on tenure. In the new hire's first quarter with the company, the overall mission is to help him get assimilated into the company's environment. As measurement of achievement, the company could provide:

- A written test on product knowledge
- A scored, mock sales call
- A scored, mock sales presentation
- Review of their business/territory plan

Based on the sales person's performance on these (relative to the SBO), he receives a percentage of the $3,750 up to 100%. At the beginning of each quarter, the sales person has a formal performance review. During the review, the quarter's results are reviewed and the next quarter's SBO is presented. The SBO plan evolves from quarter to quarter based on the tenure of the sales person and the needs of the business. The SBO is not a "gimme." 100% accomplishment should be a stretch goal, yet still achievable by the sales people.

After the first quarter, a points system is put in place, making the SBO entirely objective. The SBO program is designed by identifying key, measurable sales activities aligned with the needs of the business. Place weighting on the activities commensurate with your expectations of the sales person. In each quarter, set a 100-point goal for the sales people to achieve.

In this example, the second quarter SBO is is focused on sales pipeline development with an objective to conduct 20 face-to-face meetings with qualified prospects – a strategy to build their sales pipeline. Thus, the SBO compensates five points for each meeting conducted. At the end of the quarter, whatever percentage the sales person achieves of the 100 points, with a minimum of 75% attainment, is paid as the SBO bonus. What about those who exceed 100% of goal? Create an additional bonus for them. Why penalize them for doing more of the right things that benefit your business?

What about quality of these meetings? How do you know if they are doing the right things in the prospect meeting? Hopefully, you measured their proficiency during the first quarter. However, a great way to monitor quality is through sales pipeline management. Review sales pipelines for both new account additions and forward movement of those already on the list. If the sales person is succeeding with the SBO program, you should see both of those aspects progressing.

Perhaps, you are probably thinking, *"No way, I pay for results!"* Results are a function of your sales people doing the right things each and every day. Results are not miraculous, but rather formulaic. The reality is that you and the sales people have skin in the game with the SBO program. As a small business owner, you and your leadership team are tasked with determining what it takes for sales people to generate the desired results. If you have done your job of identifying the right success metrics and the sales people achieve those, the results take care of themselves. One important key is to budget enough dollars for the SBO bonus that it gets the attention of the sales people, but not so high that it overshadows the earning of commissions.

The bottom line is that the SBO program gives you the tools you need to channel the energy of the sales team toward achieving the business objective. It also provides you with a mechanism to attract sales talent to your company where, right on day one, they need to perform to earn dollars above their salary. The small business owner, in this example, knows that if he paid a sales person a $15,000 SBO bonus in year one, year's two and beyond are going to be stellar.

10 Steps to Sales Compensation Plan Design Success

1. Determine your business objectives as they pertain to the sales team to select the metrics you want to affect. (i.e., grow new business by $5MM)

2. Identify the critical sales activities that lead to the business objective being met. (i.e., needs analysis meetings)

3. Develop a sales metric management system that correlates sales activities with the desired results. (i.e., 10 needs analysis meetings lead to 1 sale with an average sale size of $1MM)

4. Document the frequency needed of those sales activities to generate the desired results. (i.e., 20 needs analysis meetings per rep)

5. Allocate commission dollars for your SBO plan to focus the team on the desired activities.

6. Create multiple financial models showing varying levels of sales performance and how those results affect the company and the sales team.

7. Apply the results of the model to your existing team's earnings to identify under/over performance concerns and change accordingly.

8. Review the message communicated by the plan to ensure it aligns with the business objectives. (i.e., we want new business!)

9. Compare the sales manager's compensation plan to the team's plan to ensure it is not in conflict.

10. Apply the Sales Compensation Equilateral Triangle™ (SCET™) Model to ensure all sides are balanced.

Remember, the sales compensation plan put in the hands of your sales team serves as their marching orders. Take the time to design the plan that sends your team on a quest to achieve the results you desire!

Lee B. Salz is a sales management strategist specializing in helping companies build scalable, high-performance sales organizations through hiring the right sales people, on-boarding them effectively and efficiently, and aligning their sales activities with business objectives using his sales architecture® methodology. He is the President of Sales Architects, C.E.O. of Business Expert Webinars and author of two widely-acclaimed books Soar Despite Your Dodo Sales Manager *and* Stop Speaking for Free! The Ultimate Guide to Making Money with Webinars. *Lee is also a featured columnist for* SalesForceXP *magazine and host of* The Sales Management Minute. *Lee can be reached at lsalz@SalesArchitects.net or 763.416.4321.*

9 | Networking Best Practices

Face to Face - Belly to Belly

By Cindy Cohen

As a small business owner, have you noticed the way you are doing business doesn't work anymore? Do you feel the rules have changed and no one told you? What are these changes? The way business is done has changed from old fashioned selling to relationship marketing. Now the "point of sale" is the relationship that is developed with the first meeting and with each repeated contact. Today we are unclear of whom to trust. This can feed into a growing skepticism with every business transaction; therefore, we do business with those whom we like, trust, and respect. The work environment has changed to contracted services, home-based businesses, cubical stations and less socializing. These changes can cause networking to feel at best awkward, and at worst, tortuous. For networking to be easy, fun and profitable, mastery of a specific set of skills is required. Skills and techniques are important; however, nothing is more important than to remain authentic and consistent with your personality, while relying on your strengths and personal style.

What is networking and how can you make it work for your small business?

If you ask 10 different people what networking is, you will get 10 different answers depending upon to whom you speak and their use of networking. Everyone has a network of people also known as your "circle of influence"; these include your family, friends, and business acquaintances. These are all people whom you ask for opinions, advice, and use as a daily resource. When was the last time you searched for a doctor? Did you start contacting people you know for recommendations? When you see a good movie, do you give your friends your recommendation? In your day-to-day interactions you utilize this personal network to expand your business.

Business to business networking includes the exchange of information, experience, and connections. Business networking is developing a personal connection to build supportive relationships based on mutual interests and respect which results in reciprocal benefits. To utilize networking for business leads and referrals, it requires the user to have a set of skills which include a purpose and a desired outcome. Networking can be done over the phone, through email, discussion groups, or social networking websites such as, Facebook, LinkedIn, and Twitter. However, the best networking is done in person.

To be successful and to receive the benefits of networking you need to attain a specific skill set. Since these are learned skills, everybody has the ability to *network for fun and profit*. As with all learning experiences knowledge, practice, trial and error are all required. How you apply your networking skills will determine your results. The more you practice, the more skillful you become ... leading you to better results. Networking is an ongoing, non-stop process that creates connections that last a lifetime. Networking promotes the exchange of information which strengthens relationships, builds trust, and mutual admiration with those who are in your network of contacts.

Networking builds and maximizes your "circle of influence." The average person has approximately 250 people in their "circle of influence" also called the "warm market." When you meet someone new, you gain access to their "warm market" and before you know it, you have entrance to another 250 people. When networking is approached the right way, the opportunities for your future are endless. By growing your network, you are connecting to new business, enjoying increased profitability and creating a "network community." What is a "network community?" A "network community" is filled with strategic alliances, business partner relationships and co-marketing opportunities to help you and others create successful businesses. This community of relationships, over time, evolves into friendships. Why is building friendships within your network so important? Because friends want to help friends be successful. Your networking partners/friends will help you by generating leads and referrals, developing warm contact lists, and most importantly, creating win-win relationships.

You don't feel comfortable in large groups?

That's ok! Begin by using your networking skills with one person, such as over coffee, or in a small business meeting then move on to a larger gathering such as a Chamber of Commerce event. The skills are all the same, however, the way you apply them is different. I am often asked how I developed such a large network. Where did I meet all of these people? I believe there are great networking opportunities wherever you go. If there are people, then there is a networking opportunity. As a small business owner and entrepreneur, you will be promoting your business on a continual basis. You may ask yourself, "Do I get a day off?" What I say to you is this, "If you love what you do, are you really working?"

Formal networking associations such as Business Networking International, Rainmakers, and local referral groups are always looking for new members and are waiting for your call. You can locate these organizations by performing an internet search for "networking" or "leads" or "referral groups."

The real question should be "Where can't you network?" Some additional suggestions for networking opportunities include:

- Professional organizations
- Volunteer activities: American Cancer Society
- Civic clubs & groups: Rotary, Optimist International
- Places of worship
- Kids activities: sports teams, playdates
- Hobbies: crafts, sewing, ceramics
- Recreational Activities: athletics, camping, dance class, organized sports

How does business etiquette affect networking?

Business etiquette provides guidelines on acceptable behavior and good manners in business situations. Not only should you practice proper etiquette within your own "warm market," but applying good behavior and good manners consistently will help you in all networking scenarios. I am sure you have noticed that rudeness has become a common occurrence at business meetings; however, the definition of bad behavior has not changed, even though the rules of etiquette seemed to have vanished. During business meetings and appointments be attentive, courteous, and a good listener. How many times have you heard, "Wait a minute, I have to get this message." Make the person you are with feel important. Keep your attention on the task at hand without interruption. Outside of an emergency, phone calls, voice mails, text messages, and emails should wait to be addressed post-appointment. If not, excuse yourself and walk away to address the situation. Etiquette may seem old fashioned; however, you should never feel embarrassed, or uncomfortable while knowing and following the rules of etiquette.

Is developing rapport important?

Yes, very important! Remember the last person you met and you experienced an instant connection with? You "clicked" and there was "chemistry." This is rapport. Rapport is mutual trust, connection, and understanding of another person. By establishing rapport others will want to spend more time with you. What happens when you meet someone you don't like? Do the other person's qualities seem insincere, dishonest, or mistrusting in someway? Not only do you not want to be around them, you don't want to help them, or want help from them. On the other hand, if we like someone and feel comfortable around them, we tend to be generous and go out of our way to help them. Being a good conversationalist is part of developing rapport because it helps others feel at ease. Looking for instant rapport? Make eye contact, smile, and have a firm, effective handshake, listen, be supportive, attentive, respectful, and give genuine compliments.

What should be in your networking tool box?

Your networking tool box consists of tools that create effective connections. Now is a good time to design your networking tool box and be ready to put it to use at any given moment.

Tool Box Supplies include:

1. **Business Cards** – Your business card is a "mini billboard" advertisement. Your business card provides a brief statement about you and a description of your service or product. When you have your business card with you, it is like saying "I'm open for business."

2. **Name Tag** – A name tag will help others remember your name for introductions and will broadcast your business. You will be surprised at how much business you can "cook up" at your local grocery store by wearing a name tag. If someone is not wearing their name tag, and you forgot their name, simply say, "I'm sorry, your name escapes me," or "I'm _____, please tell me my name again." This is a polite way to respond to an awkward situation and these introductions work every time.

3. **Your Story** – Your story is your advertisement to the world and how you connect to others. You may have heard the terms "elevator speech," "60 second commercial" or "unique selling point." These presentation methods are designed as guidelines to help you introduce yourself in a concise manner. Your presentation should include your name, product or services you

offer and what differentiates you from similar companies. Be able to state your "commercial" at the spur of the moment without hesitation, in a friendly, warm, and confident manner.

4. **Calendar Schedule** – Networking provides you with the setting to make your first introduction and your scheduled appointment is the second step. At the appointment you learn how to help connect, provide and receive referrals. Following-up or staying connected in a timely manner after your initial meeting is extremely important. Know your schedule so the time between your initial meeting and your second meeting is kept to a minimum because you want your new contact to remember who you are.

5. **Send a Card** – Networking isn't a "one night stand!" Communication holds any relationship together. After networking, connect through telephone, email, social networking websites, and appointments. A hand written card will always set you apart from your competition.

How to put your best foot forward?

Networking increases your visibility, which comes with scrutiny. You only get one chance to make a first impression, so make sure you look and feel your best. Be your own judge and evaluate yourself. Review how you entered the room: did you stand up straight and make eye contact; did you look friendly with a big (show your teeth) smile, say "Hello" and give your name; and did you end your conversation with a firm handshake? What were you wearing? A clean, neat and conservative overall appearance is best. It's better to be overdressed than underdressed. Women should dress modestly and men should wear a suit or button down shirt with a jacket and slacks. Consult your local library or bookstore for specific "dress for success" guidelines.

Are you looking and feeling your best? Do you take care of yourself? It is hard to be your best when you are feeling run down, sick or tired. Remember the last time you felt too "tired" to network? Did that cost you money? Good health is good for you and your business. Since you are your business, keeping yourself in the "game" by improving your health, helps your business to thrive.

Three health habits to increase your performance, reduce stress, and increase your energy are:

1. **Make Healthy Food Choices** - Eat more fruits, vegetables, fish, and whole grains. Consuming the right foods will reduce sickness, increase energy, stamina, vitality and the health you need to give you, and your business the best chance for success. Medical studies and experts agree the daily intake for optimal health includes approximately 5 - 6 cups of fruits and vegetables, and 35 grams of fiber and a ratio of 2:1 of good fats. Now, what's on your plate?

2. **Exercise & Physical Activity** - Exercising increases your quality of life by improving mood, sleep, reducing appetite and risks for disease. If you can't join a gym, then exercise in your living room, basement, or backyard or go for a walk. There are great websites to help you whether you're a beginner or an expert in fitness. If you don't have a lot of time, exercise in 5 minute increments. Over a lifetime those 5 minutes add up.

3. **Sleep & Rest** - During sleep the body heals itself, reducing stress, processing information gathered during the day, and rejuvenating the mind and body. Ways to develop good sleeping habits include: going to bed at a consistent time, turning off all electronics, not eating 3 hours before bedtime, reducing your consumption of caffeinated, sugary food, and drinking water throughout the day.

The handshake -- is it really that important?

The handshake says "Let's be friends." When being introduced to someone new, stand up and offer your hand to shake, look the person in the eye, smile and say their name. With the quality (firmness) of your handshake comes an evaluation of your confidence and character. Not shaking hands can be perceived negatively. Conversely, it can positively impact the advancement of your career and business. In the United States, extending your hand in friendship communicates, "I want to be friends with you."

Four handshake classifications:

1. **Hand to Hand Shake** – This standard handshake extends right hand to right hand. A firm grasp (not too hard) and shake leaves the best impression. This is the preferred hand shake with business acquaintances.

2. **Two Handed Shake** – Both hands are used, which communicates a friendly and warm greeting. This is the handshake between friends.

3. **Elbow Hand Shake** – The right hand is extended to shake hands, and the left hand is placed on the recipients elbow. This technique is frequently employed by men who are very friendly with each other. It's a handshake – hug. If you are a man, avoid this handshake when greeting women. It may be perceived as "too" friendly.

4. **Dead Fish Handshake** – This handshake is "loosey goosey," and is also described as the "dead fish" handshake. This hand shake leaves the impression of lack in confidence and unprofessionalism. To avoid this handshake, practice with a friend and get constructive feedback.

Did you introduce yourself?

Business introductions can be awkward. Remember the last event you attended when you stood there waiting to be introduced? Did you feel the longer you waited the more "invisible" you became? No networking is happening here! The alternative is to introduce yourself. How should you do that? Wait for a break in the conversation and then clearly state your name and your company, followed by "It's a pleasure to meet you," then ask a question such as "Would you mind telling me about you and about what you do?" or "I would love to hear something exciting that happened to you this week ... what would that be?" Now you're off and running.

Why is starting a conversation so difficult?

For most of us our number one fear is public speaking. The fear behind public speaking is caused by exposing ourselves to the possibility of rejection and embarrassment. Starting a conversation is a form of public speaking, thus it can be just as anxiety provoking. What's behind the fear? When we were young we were taught, "Don't talk to strangers," and "Wait until you are properly introduced," or "Children should be seen and not heard." What distortions did you hear as a child that may be hurting you now? Parents mean well; however, these messages impact the way you interact with friends, do business, and relate to the world. For me, once I realized everyone was just as fearful of starting a conversation as I was, it made talking with them easier. Knowing we are all afraid meant I needed only to be a little less afraid than those I met in order to get the conversation going. To be successful you may want to transition to positive internal thoughts such as "I'm safe, trusting, and open to new ideas."

There's a formula to a valuable conversation. Once you learn how, it's pretty much the same every time. The first step is to "break the ice" and once this is achieved you are on your way. Here are examples of good ice-breakers to get the other person talking:

> *Hi, my name is Cindy Cohen, I am a nurse, and I own my own my own health and wellness company. I teach others how to be healthy.*

> *What is your name? Who do you work for?*

> *Do you own your own company? What do you do there?*

The next step is to learn to ask good questions to continue the conversation. Be prepared with a list of questions until you feel comfortable being "spontaneous." Open ended questions demonstrate your level of interest and elicit the biggest response. You will know your question was not open ended when the response is a "yes" or "no." This is a definite conversation stopper.

Examples of open-ended questions:

- How has networking grown your business?
- How did you start your business?
- What was the biggest challenge you faced as a business owner?

Are you a stay at home mom? Try this:

- What's the best part of being at home with your children?
- What do you find the most challenging and rewarding?

Communication and perceptions come from what you say and don't say during a conversation. The words you choose have less to do with how others perceive you, and more to do with your facial expressions and body language. Perceptions are formed in 3 ways: what is said (verbal cues), what isn't said (non-verbal cues), and what isn't seen (visual cues). During your next conversation, utilize a self-monitoring process by asking yourself the following questions:

- Am I actively listening or thinking about something else?
- Am I standing too close?
- Do I have good posture?
- Do I have a smile on my face?

Are you interesting to talk to? To make interesting conversation, you must appear interesting. Creating meaningful conversation is the essence of networking. Become interesting to talk to by brushing up on current events, your field, and interesting topics. Avoid the "water-cooler" topics such as sex, politics, and religion. Remember, money making is created by forming valuable relationships through meaningful conversation while networking.

How to end the conversation at a networking event?

Ending a conversation can be awkward, but it doesn't have to be. Everyone at the event is there to create new contacts and reconnect with others. To end a conversation, include an exit comment that is positive and sincere in the past tense such as, "It's been great meeting you, I look forward to getting together with you next week over coffee." Never cut someone off, give a reason for the departure, be honest, excuse yourself and remember to shake hands.

Did you evaluate your last networking experience?

Congratulations for successfully surviving one, two, or maybe many networking events! It wasn't too bad, was it? The best time to evaluate your networking experience is immediately following the event. Ask yourself, how did I present myself? Was I prepared? Did I ask for their business card? How were my introduction, hand shake, and conversation? Was I authentic, pleasant, friendly, kind and helpful? Evaluate your behavior from the other persons' point of view. Congratulate yourself on a good job and remember to make follow-up appointments. Without following up, the networking event is just another party, not a business building event.

Have not seen you in a while, where did you go?

It is a big mistake to stop networking. When you stop being seen around town, you disappear. In today's economic climate this could be deadly to your business. "Here today, gone tomorrow" is definitely true. Always keep your calendar full of face-to-face networking and continue to see and be seen! Networking is an effective way to exchange ideas, information, talents and experience. Networking doesn't increase your bottom line instantly, but over time it brings value to your networking community, company and life. Networking is a particular skill set which includes the rules of etiquette, developing rapport, shaking hands, having an effective conversation, making connections, listening, and following up with those you meet.

Modifications, adjustments, and recognition are all part of the evaluation process to your success. Mastering networking skills creates a community of people who can help you increase your business connections, profitability, develop your career, and grow life long friendships while having fun.

Cindy Cohen is recognized as a networking thought leader ... networking for fun and profit. As the Founder of C2 Your Health, Cindy combined her two passions, health and business, to build a health and wellness firm though face-to-face networking. She has also used her networking expertise to become an award-winning National Marketing Director with the Juice Plus Corporation, whole food based nutrition made from 17 different fruits, vegetables and grains (YourJuicePlus.com). She has also built four successful networking groups and shares her networking concepts through both coaching and training. Cindy can be reached through her websites: CindyCohenNetworking.com and C2YourHealthNow.com; or email cindycohenrn@yahoo.com.

10 | Sales Intelligence Secrets

Know More Selling

By Sam Richter

The Internet has changed the way companies sell, and buyers buy. Unless you have been living on a deserted island for the past 15 years, I know that statement did not send shock waves through your consciousness. And even if you had been living on a deserted island, you probably had Internet access anyhow. However, I am not talking about companies selling their products online, and consumer online purchases continuing to grow annually by double-digits.

Rather, I am talking about business-to-business selling. No... not reverse auctions, online catalogs, and the ability to leverage the Internet for global outsourcing. I am talking about the traditional sales person calling on a prospect or even an existing client — the one-on-one client relationship — that the Internet has completely redefined.

Unfortunately, most salespeople do not yet fully grasp the scope of change. Nor have they grasped the opportunities it represents to the companies and salespeople who understand HOW to leverage the Internet to grow their traditional sales business.

For most complex product and service sales, there is no doubt that the role of the salesperson has, and always will be, integral to the deal-closing process. People still buy from people that they like and trust. The ability for the salesperson to understand the prospect or client, ask probing questions that get to the heart of business issues, and create relevant solutions that ultimately deliver results is core to every sales program and sales process.

Big companies spend millions of dollars each year on sales training. They teach various techniques for getting past gatekeepers, identifying buyer advocates, and interacting with decision makers. At the core of all good sales training programs is a section that discusses how imperative it is to understand your customers, their needs, their business issues, and as some programs call it, their "pain."

The problem is, in today's world where virtually everyone is exceptionally pressed for time, there is an expectation by many buyers that sales people know the answers to questions *BEFORE* they walk in the door (or pick up the phone or send an email). Especially for in-person meetings, buyers get frustrated when a salesperson asks what some feel are obvious questions like company size, lines of business, competitive information, etc. Many buyers expect salespeople — even in the first meeting — to have even more complex business knowledge such as industry changes, market positioning, and even a base-level understanding of the buyer's internal business issues.

How can you get the kinds of information that will make a great first impression? How can you differentiate from the typical salesperson? How can you get the information you need to understand your prospect and their key issues before you walk in the door? The answer is Sales Intelligence.

The Power of Sales Intelligence and the "Fourth R"

According to a 2007 study by CSO Insights, Sales Intelligence is one of the most effective tools for improving a salesperson's, and a company's, sales effectiveness. When a salesperson understands the prospect; the company, the industry focus, the issues being faced, and details about the individual with whom the salesperson is meeting, then the salesperson is able to customize the presentation and conduct a meaningful sales call. In fact, according to a CSO Insights study, if your company embraces a culture of Sales Intelligence and if your salespeople have access to meaningful information, your company is almost two times more likely to move your prospects through your sales process towards a closed deal (regardless of which sales process you use) versus sales organizations with difficult or no access to this type of information. Said another way, if you know how to find and use information, you will win two times more business than the competitors that "wing it."

Yet, according to the CSO Insight study, fewer than 10% of companies provide their sales reps the training and resources necessary to conduct Sales Intelligence. Why?

Historically, students of business and sales are taught that success comes from mastering the traditional "Three Rs" of reading, writing, and arithmetic. If you learn to communicate effectively, write a good proposal, understand a financial spreadsheet, and manage a realistic budget, the chances are good that you will succeed in business.

In today's value-oriented business marketplace, the "Fourth R" – research – is the tool that truly differentiates one business from the next and one salesperson from the next. Talk with anyone who is an expert at influencing people, from a minister to a politician to a great salesperson, and they all practice the "Fourth R." If you understand what interests the people you meet with, if you know what they genuinely care about, you can ask relevant questions and engage people to share what they most likely do not share with others.

In *How to Win Friends and Influence People*, Dale Carnegie shares a story about President Theodore Roosevelt and his adherence to practicing the "Fourth R" prior to meeting with people. Carnegie writes about Roosevelt:

> *Everyone who was ever a guest of Theodore Roosevelt was astonished at the range and diversity of his knowledge. Whether his visitor was a cowboy or a Rough Rider, a New York politician or a diplomat, Roosevelt knew what to say. And how was it done? The answer was simple. Whenever*

Roosevelt expected a visitor, he sat up late the night before, reading up on the subject in which he knew his guest was particularly interested. For Roosevelt knew, as all leaders know, that the royal road to a person's heart is to talk about things he or she treasures most.

If the former president of the United States could practice the "Fourth R," you certainly can now. If you say that you do not have the time to conduct research on your prospects, I would challenge you to look at your daily calendar and imagine comparing it to the calendar of Roosevelt. The question you need to ask yourself is, "Do I want to be good at what I do, or do I want to be known as one of the best?"

Instead of generic questions, the "Fourth R" will help you tailor questions and establish your credibility in ways that are more likely to elicit a response. By having an informed understanding of the issues your prospect is most likely facing before you begin a meeting, you will be able to ask relevant questions that are more likely to generate a meaningful response.

Imagine the dialogue you could engage in if you knew your prospect's annual revenue growth, the trends in your prospect's industry, how your prospect's competitors are performing, new products your prospect is introducing into the marketplace, and even how your prospect's customers are doing and the issues they face.

When you are armed with relevant data, you are able to not only ask better questions, but you also massively increase your credibility. Remember, people buy from people. People buy from people they trust. And people trust people who can intelligently engage in dialogue that is relevant.

Asking a generic question like: "What are the key barriers to you achieving your objectives?" shows your prospect that you are a trained salesperson. Asking a prospect a question like, "I see that your biggest competitor, Widget Corporation, is coming out with a new product and I was wondering how you plan to differentiate yourself?", shows your prospect that you are a sales professional who understands the market.

The "Fourth R" is a powerful tool that, once applied in every sales interaction, will elevate you to the top one percent of all salespeople. The good news is that virtually anyone can learn to master the "Fourth R." You don't have to attend library school. You don't need a private investigator's license. You just have to follow a few simple steps.

How the Impersonal Web has Made
Selling More Personal

Admit it; the Internet has made you a lazier salesperson. Instead of calling, you email. Instead of in-person meetings, you hold a Web chat. Instead of truly understanding your prospects and clients, you look at their Web page.

Remember earlier, I discussed how the Web has changed the world for the traditional relationship-based salesperson, but most salespeople do not comprehend the magnitude. That is because what the Web has done, is made it fast and easy to practice the "Fourth R."

When used for Sales Intelligence purposes, the impersonal Web makes it easier to be more personal. Via the Web, you can quickly find the information you need to craft relevant presentations, pitches, and proposals to help you interact with prospects and clients in ways you know are *meaningful to them*. **To find the right information, you just have to know where and how to look.**

Searching for information online can be very frustrating. Popular search engines like Google and Bing continue to make amazing strides in their ability to gather information. They have added tens of millions of Web pages to their databases and introduced new search features that make finding information easier and more personal. New search engines seem to launch every week, each with a new way to locate and display search results.

Yet with all of the advances made in search technology, finding relevant, credible, and timely information online is challenging and time-consuming for most people. Many people, even those who have grown up using the Internet, have little knowledge of how to conduct efficient searches and, thus, waste an incredible amount of time searching for business information.

Following are a few of the resources featured in the breakthrough, top-selling and award-winning book, *Take the Cold Out of Cold Calling* (www.takethecold.com). Combined with the Know More! Center with its Downloadable Toolbar (www.warmcallcenter.com), when you use these tips, tricks and resources, you will be well on your way to mastering Sales Intelligence, and winning more business than you ever thought possible.

- **Google Filetype Search:** From company proposals to vendor and client lists, companies think that the files they post online for colleagues to download are secure. But if not properly protected, Google can index the data and make it available to people who know how to look.

    1. Enter the information you want and/or the company name (use quotations around phrases e.g. "paper industry" or "Widget Corporation").

    2. Enter filetype: (filetype colon) and then choose a filetype extension e.g. pdf = adobe acrobat; xls = Excel spreadsheets; ppt = PowerPoint document; doc = Word document. For example…

        ◊   **"Paper industry" + "membership list" filetype:xls** will search for a paper industry membership list in Excel format.

        ◊   **"Widget Corporation" filetype:ppt** will search for a Widget Corporation PowerPoint presentation.

        ◊   **"Plastics industry" + trends OR issues filetype:pdf** will locate research reports and/or articles related to trends or issues in the plastics industry.

- **Google Options:** Type the name of a company or a person in Google. For the best search results, make sure to put the name within quotes (e.g. "Acme Corporation" or "Sam Richter").

    On the Google results page, on the left side, you'll notice a number of options. Click the "More" link to expand the options. You can use these options to sort your search results by

Type. Click the "News" link to get current and archived news articles related to your search. Clicking on the "Blogs" link delivers mentions of your search term(s) in blogs. Clicking "Updates" shows you real-time Twitter, Facebook, and other micro-blog and instant updates results. You can literally find out what people are saying about a company or person *at that very moment!*

After you click on a Type, you can further sort your results by date range. Click the "Past Year," "Past Week," or "Past 24 Hours" links to limit your results to articles and information that has appeared within those time frames.

Click the smaller "More Search Tools" link. One of the options is labeled "Timeline." Click on the link and you will see a graphical timeline by decade, with certain time periods blocked out. Click on one of the blocked out periods and you will see a graphical timeline by year during that decade, with the search results only showing information about the company from that year. Click a blocked out year and you can see a graphical timeline by month, with the search results showing information that is related to that specific month in that specific year.

How can you use this information? Imagine prior to a sales call that you conduct this sort of search. You click on the current month and pull up press releases and articles. You reference this information during your meeting, for example, you might say: "I saw in your company press release from last week that you are ..." or "I thought that article from last month where you were quoted was ..." Click on "Latest" link and you might even be able to say something like "congratulations on winning that new piece of business...this morning."

Find out what was going on at the company or what a person was doing in the past, and what they are currently doing, and you can ask poignant questions. Read the information carefully and relate what you find to shared experiences in your career.

- **Manta.com:** You have probably heard about Dun & Bradstreet and its company information databases. You have also probably heard that D&B is fairly expensive. Did you know there is a free service from the Website Manta, that with registration, provides basic D&B data?

Type in the name of a company into the search form, and choose the correct company from the results list. You will find basic company information including location and industry; plus additional data including the number of employees, revenue figures, year started, key executives, and more.

Bookmark Manta on your mobile phone and use it a few minutes prior to each meeting. Refresh your memory about a company and use the information to ask great questions and share your knowledge.

- **Referenceforbusiness.com/industries (Encyclopedia of American Industries):** Imagine the next sales meeting where you share industry statistics and knowledge that your buyer might not even have. Do you think your credibility will reach a new high?

  You can quickly get an overview of just about every industry by using the online Encyclopedia of American Industries database. Once on the site, click on a category and then scroll down to find the appropriate sub-category or SIC code. You can also use the search engine by entering the industry you would like to learn about. Click on a result and get an industry overview complete with impressive statistics.

- **ZoomInfo.com:** Want an easy way to find an executive's biography? ZoomInfo scours the Web locating information on people, and then automatically creates an online biography using the information that it found.

  To use, click the "people" tab and enter the first and last name of the person you are interested in finding. If the name is a common name (e.g. Pat Smith), use advanced search when on the people section, and enter in additional terms such as the company where the person works.

- **LinkedIn.com:** This social networking site is a great way to research people, and even receive virtual referrals and recommendations—the most powerful kind of marketing. Once you are registered, invite people into your network. Your network grows exponentially because as people accept your invitations, and you accept theirs, everyone's network is shared. As your network grows, search for people by name, company, job title and more. Use the Advanced Search for the best results.

  Following a search, if you see a name of someone you are interested in learning about, click their name and view their LinkedIn profile. Each person creates his or her own online profile, so you can learn a lot about someone's background and interests, as you are basically looking at their online resume.

  If you find someone you would like to meet, you can request a referral from one of your first level contacts—just click the "Get Introduced By a Connection" link. Choose the person you know who knows the person you would like to meet. Write both a note, and LinkedIn will facilitate the online introduction.

- **Pipl.com:** Pipl is one of the most comprehensive, free, people search sites you'll find. Pipl searches hundreds of sources to compile results, many of which are not searched by popular search engines.

  Enter a person's name and city or state, and in a few seconds, Pipl will aggregate information it found from social networks, Web pages, blogs, court records, and even PDF files like articles, annual reports, white papers, etc. featuring your prospects or client's name.

  On many people, Pipl provides a Quick Fact result section that allows you to get facts about the person's career, educational background, and more. Pipl sometimes provides business and even home contact information, including email addresses and phone numbers.

- **Your Local Library:** Most people are not aware of this, but one of the most powerful business research resources around is your local public library. Big companies with big budgets pay for expensive databases and list building services. What you probably do not realize is most libraries have the same or similar databases that you can use.

  Best of all, you can access these databases free of charge (well...they are not exactly free because your tax dollars paid for them). Even better is you can often access most of these databases at no charge via your own home or work computer, any time you'd like. Just find your library's Website; for a listing, visit the Warm Call Center and click "Your Library." Once on your library's site, locate a tab or link titled "databases" or "online resources." Click on the link to access the database and enter in your library card number. In seconds you'll be logged into premium subscription databases at no charge to you or your company.

- **WarmCallCenter.com:** Visit the Warm Call Center, register, and access the Invisible Web company, industry, and people section so you can easily practice the "Fourth R." Even better, you can download the Warm Call Toolbar and access these people search sites directly from your Web browser...you'll literally be two clicks away from information on just about anybody.

Follow these tips and resources and you will be well on your way to mastering the "Fourth R" and Sales Intelligence. Most important, you will begin to know more than you ever thought you could (or should) about your prospects, clients, and your competition.

Sam Richter is an internationally recognized expert on Sales Intelligence. His top-selling book, Take the Cold Out of Cold Calling *is in multiple editions and has received numerous accolades. Sam is an internationally sought-after presenter and is founder of the Know More! business improvement program (www.samrichter.com). Sam is the former president of a national business research organization, is a member of the Business Journal's Forty Under 40, and has been s a finalist for Inc. Magazine's Entrepreneur of the Year.*

11 | Lead Generation

Techniques to Increase Your Sales Pipeline

By Drew Stevens, Ph.D.

According to CSO Insights, "Sales Performance Optimization 2009 Survey Results and Analysis," an astonishing 54% of 1,800 firms fail to turn leads into a meeting more than half of the time. For any small business owner, this is the primary stumbling block. If your sales team can't get you in the door of a prospective client ... how can your company survive? Effective lead generation is your most powerful component to increasing sales productivity.

The current rules of business have changed significantly as a result of constantly updated technology and the relentless strain on time management. Organizations must become more nimble to the needs of clients and much more efficient with selling effectiveness. Too much labor is involved with issues other than producing leads. Too little time is spent with economic buyers and establishing value based relationships. The hub of selling effectiveness requires lead generation, not only getting them into the pipeline, but through it!

There are Three Lead Generation Strategies:
- **Prospecting Opportunities**
- **Value Based Selling**
- **Process Selling**

Prospecting Opportunities - Is There Gold in Those Names?

Contacts for business are similar to gold bullion in a stream. Consumer buying processes are altered with the proliferation of technology and global communication. Clients now know more information about the company and basics prior to the first contact.

The requirement is that businesses and their peers get into the sales game sooner. The longer it takes to establish contact, the larger the gap and easier for clients to find competitors. Value must be presented quickly or otherwise conversations are lost.

Cold calling, direct mail and other traditional selling methods do little to build relationships. When was the last time you took a call in the evening after a lengthy day from a cold calling manic? When conducting workshops and consulting, I advocate that before a selling professional picks up a telephone and states, "Hello," they must have information on whom they are calling. Sales Intelligence requires the use of industry information and proper research to understand information on the company, its chief competitors, and the industry. A review of current customers and issues affecting the company are useful since the content can be used to drive discussion with the economic buyer. Another interesting perspective is that sellers are outsiders and they see trends and threats customers might not.

The most bountiful sources of company information come directly from annual reports, national newspapers and even the Internet. A simple Google search helps those searching for client information with a wealth of content. There are databases such as Sorkins© and Leadership Directories© that offer content rich profiles.[1] The information on company, competition and products/services is used to drive discussion.

---

1   I make no compensation from these. There are other similar databases which are also used as examples. Many of these points may already be familiar.

Not all People are Created Equal

Another helpful lead generation technique is targeting and segmenting your markets. These need to be done with the utmost thought and rigor. Target market selection is an imperative tactic of selling. You need to know who your best potential clients are.

Targeting assists with dissecting the total population of potential clients into a microcosm of those most possible to speak with. Similar to the manner of moving leads through the pipeline, target market selection creates a subset of possibilities. There are four methods to dividing the market:

1. **Geographic segmentation** – Location specific. Lead generation is produced by choosing a location within 100 miles of the corporation's headquarters; thus, enabling better customer service and customer interaction.

2. **Demographic segmentation** – Measurable statistics include, but are not limited to, age, race, sex, religion, ethnicity, and income, etc. Conversations related to products and services are aided with better comprehension of client's values and perspective.

3. **Psychographic segmentation** – Lifestyle preferences and their attitudes, interests, and desires. As buyers detail preferences, the conversations immediately relate to value. Competitive differentiation is vital here.

4. **Behavioristic segmentation** – Values and beliefs and desired benefits. Conversations are stimulated by focusing on the benefits that relate to customer needs.

In addition to the strategies above, here are some tactical elements to assist in lead generation.

Low Hanging Fruit

We know so many individuals, yet we do not tap into the vital resources that can aid us. Sometimes seeking business opportunities is as simple as calling a friend or removal from the comfort zone to walk over to your neighbor's home. Business requires chutzpah! You have two choices: 1. You can sit behind a desk pondering how to get business or 2. Step up in front of someone's desk requesting it!

Networking

Truly the best professionals constantly network. Good professionals by nature require constant engagement with others to comprehend business trends and meet new opportunities. For over 27 years, I have attended at least one or two networking events per month and I can attribute a number of leads and new clients to this practice. Admittedly, there exist a plethora of networking associations and organizations. Choose those close to your location and aligned with your business. How can anyone know your business with just a shingle hanging in the breeze?

Referrals

Proper networking and sales etiquette involves referral acquisition. Similar to gaining closure agreement many professionals abhor asking for the order! Business is driven by the ability to ask for new business. If clients are happy with your work they will gladly and willingly provide you with referrals. The best way to seek referrals is when you are first engaged with the client and they are in that emotional high. More importantly, you want to ask when you are in the account, since this is the best time to be top of mind.

Another imperative item to remember – there is strength in numbers – the more referrals you obtain, the fuller the pipeline. There is a story of an insurance professional who would visit clients and not leave without three new referrals. Even if the client provided one or two, the agent would not leave until he received three or more. Remember this is the easiest part of the lead generation process ... ask for your referrals.

Follow Up on Referrals

It might seem pragmatic, yet there is much evidence to illustrate that many professionals do not follow up. Friends, family, and current clients typically provide these golden nuggets so it is vital that follow up occur. A rule of thumb is twenty-four hours from receipt to contact.

There are many valuable activities for small business owners to improve lead generation. How many are you engaged in now?

Speaking

The number one fear is public speaking. Aside from cold calling it is the second most relevant way to obtain leads. Every business professional is an expert in his or her market and has something to share. Speaking is an opportunity to meet new individuals while allowing the leads to come to you.

Developing Brand

The laws of persuasion and attraction operate efficiently when the organization or its employees are branded. Individuals become persuaded by name recognition, whether an individual in an organization or the firm itself. Building your personal brand is a terrific method to create sales attraction. Do you have a sentence, a tagline or a name that can create a personal brand?

Teaching

During the draft of this book a former student approached me, "Do you have February 23rd available, I need to book you for a keynote!" That is leverage. I am an adjunct professor at universities because I love teaching, and it also helps to establish a sales funnel. Teaching is a wonderful approach to community service and a great method to generate leads. Do you have expertise in an area that can be shared with others?

Value Based Selling

The way to avoid the trap of being just a regular selling professional and a high achiever is to refrain from the traditional model of features and benefits. Look at the client in terms of outcomes and results. The visual illustrates the importance of value and partnership. No matter the issue, focus on how your organization provides the results the client seeks. It is not about facts, but the return on the client's investment.

Building your business is not about making money, but about creating the relationships and clients. The conversation with prospects should not be about features, but rather the value from you and your product/service. Do not focus on fees, commissions, costs, or any other sales related words. If the discussion is not about value, then you have surrendered control of the discussion and the result will not be in your preferred terms. I recall a great quote from a mentor, Alan Weiss Seminar:

> *"Language controls discussion, discussion controls the relationship, and relationship controls the business."*

When the conversation focuses on value, the prospect becomes convinced of the knowledge you provide and desires a relationship with you. Therefore, all discussions must focus on how working with your organization produces returns for the client with minimal investment in time and money.

Methods to Illustrate Value

Discover Objectives

Ask the client to provide three objectives they desire with the use of your services. People act on emotion; therefore, if your questions concentrate on needed objectives, especially if they apply to need, then you will create value. Prudent questions focus on future vision, future outcome, and future efficiencies. Clients today seek two things: profits and productivity. When your questions focus on client objectives, they indicate aspirations for business improvement.

Sample Questions for Objectives and Value
• Ideally, what would you like to accomplish?
• What is the ideal outcome that you want to establish?
• How will you know we've accomplished the objective?
• What does this mean to you personally?
• How will this affect performance?
• What is the intangible impact?

Additional Outcomes

In my entire business career so many automatically know what they want, but few know what they need. Ask additional questions that provide value by honing in on these differences. The focus here is on value to the organization and to the individual, as well as measurements for success.

Focus on Output, Not Input

No one cares about your creative advertising or corporate office. Demonstrate important outcomes for the client, such as speed, guarantees, high return, and transition management. When you focus on client results, conversations become crisp and tightly focused.

Listen

I recall buying a car many years ago. I was not focused on price, but rather on features. Yet most of the sales people insisted on delivering a pitch, telling me how to drive, or suggesting features that did not interest me. You cannot learn while you are talking. Develop provocative questions and keep the prospect talking until you have enough emotional and factual information to embrace them as partners. When you listen, and clients talk, you also obtain better information.

Testimonials

People like to conduct business with those whom they know and like. Begin by obtaining a testimonial from every possible client. Relationships are built based on prior expertise. Your ability to nimbly build a "book" of testimonials will assist you in becoming the provider of choice.

Decision Makers

Gatekeepers waste time and do not understand value. Gatekeepers focus on victim-hood and conceit. Decision makers concern themselves with productivity and value. Do not be confused by titles. There are many individuals who believe titles have enormous clout. 67% of business professionals spend too much time with those that cannot make a decision. Sellers are often duped into the process because they do not ask the proper questions. Good detective work means asking the difficult questions.

Process Selling – Selling is a Process; Not an Event

Clients purchase from people they like and trust. That statement is so compelling that I need to repeat it once again so that you fully understand its importance: *clients purchase from people they like and trust.* It is quite possible that they do not trust you. People want honest information about what the service can do for them. This fundamental issue is the key to selling success. Ethics are difficult to instruct – you have them or you don't!

Here are the most important rules about selling that I have learned over the years:

1. There are four simple steps (described below) of selling that are vital. You do not need numerous methods and training. Learn the four simple steps and you will sell more than you realize.
2. There is no basic selling rule or principle that has been discovered in the last hundred years.

3. You need to take these principles and use them daily. Practicing these rules and making them a habit in your daily life will make you better.

4. Do not rush learning. Rome was not built in a day. You must learn daily and practice daily but without haste and impatience.

5. Evaluate yourself. Be critical and learn by what you are doing and not doing to become better. Be honest in your assessment.

In order to achieve, you must be patient and you must have faith to become better each day.

Selling is not an overnight process. Selling is a profession that takes years to master, and even then, there is always something to learn. There is no way that in three weeks you will become proficient in selling. Nor can it occur in one sales training course. Selling, like human development, is a process that will take you years of time, energy and investment. Similar to a stock, invest in yourself, and watch the returns soar to great heights.

Four Primary Steps in the Selling Process:

1. Prepare to Present
2. Uncover the Needs
3. Manage Rapport and Objections
4. Provide Closure

I have not only used these steps but I have also instructed for well over 27 years. I have trained over 60,000 selling professionals and have helped them achieve over a half billion dollars in gross revenues. These steps have worked for them and they will work for you too!

This is what you need to know:

1. The prospect might be interested and you might have their attention, but your inability to build a relationship impacts moving forward. To that end, prospects will object to your offer. You must understand how to move forward to create further interest so they trust you!

2. Unless you are asking provocative questions and you illustrate concern for the prospect, they will go elsewhere. Uncovering needs means asking the difficult questions to understand those needs.

3. It is vital to keep your prospect's attention so they remain interested. If prospects are interested in your offer and they "hear" the benefits, they are more likely to listen and invest the time with your offer.

4. The most fascinating yet most daunting part of any sale is closure. Procrastination and indecision are a part of life. Moreover, many professionals are afraid to ask for the business. The best way to make money and get more clients is to ask.

P-R-A-C-T-I-C-E™ Selling – Your GPS To Selling

Ninety-two percent of all sales professionals do not use or have a formal selling process. This ultimately affects pipeline movement and closure ratio. Einstein once stated, "Insanity is doing the same thing continually and expecting a different result." My experience in the field and working particularly with athletes has helped me develop the process I want to introduce to you. My belief is that athletes practice to obtain strengths in performance; attorneys practice to become more efficient with litigation or servicing clients; physicians practice since the body mechanics and issues differ from person to person; and musicians practice to better harmonize. Selling is a profession that requires continuous improvement in skills and relationships as well. As consumer behavior changes, sellers need to be more efficient with handling relationships and expectations. The only method to encourage them it is to P-R-A-C-T-I-C-E™.

A Breakdown of the P-R-A-C-T-I-C-E™ Method

Planning

The most vital process for any successful professional is planning. Planning is about information gathering and research. An acronym for **PLAN** is **P**lan to **L**ive **A**nd **N**ever be unhappy. Professionals must plan each call and they must be prepared to offer information. Additionally, professionals must identify with research information to resolve the client's pains.

Rapport

Building rapport is one of the largest hurdles for any business professional. You have to get to know people, even strangers. This will challenge you daily. However, you must always be smiling and discover new ways to constantly influence people to resolve their issues.

Attention

Buyers today are much more distracted by email, voice mail, snail mail, internet, remote controls, and cell phones, etc. Professionals must rise above the static to be heard. And, more importantly, you must keep their attention so that buyers are not distracted from you. Differentiation is your key to maintain attention.

Conviction

These are the tools that you need to convince your client to buy from you. Professionals typically carry an arsenal of information for sales calls. However, each call must be customized with the tools and techniques so the buyer will "hear." Items such as testimonials, statistical studies, charts, graphs, and schematics are just some of the items you will need.

Time Management

It is imperative to work with efficiency. Good organizational and time management skills ensure your productivity and profitability.

Interest

If you want someone to buy something from you, it is imperative that you interest them. This means using tools and fact-finding techniques to determine if there is alignment with you and the prospect. And it requires the use of benefits to obtain the sale. Remember the rule – prospects buy benefits.

Close

Never forget to ask for the sale – what do you want to obtain. Closing is one of the most vital steps in the business process. If you do not close ... you do not make any money. Remember when you close – use the ABC rule; *Always be closing!*

Evaluation and Education

Be enthusiastic about your product or service. You want to love what you do and you want to love what you sell. Your interest or lack of it will be revealed through every presentation. Even though rejection rears its ugly head in the sales game, your enthusiasm must remain unyielding.

Finally, enlightenment comes with each and every call. Learn something new with every sales call and each presentation. *Business professionals must be adept at lifelong learning!*

Drew Stevens, Ph.D. is one of the world's leading authorities on business development and sales thought leadership. Dr. Drew is the author of the successful sales process book Split Second Selling. He is also the creator of the Sales Leadership Certificate. It is one of only fourteen programs in the United States offering an accredited degree in the profession of selling and has a top ranked podcast called Sales Fitness. To discover how Dr. Drew can assist your organization to increase their business development skills visit him at www.drewstevensconsulting.com.

12 Business Development

The Dynamics of Great Business Development

By Richard Norris

In this day and age, it is critical as a small business to ensure that every dollar goes farther and your time is maximized. Every penny is an investment. This particularly applies in the area of business development; regardless of whether you are a start-up or an existing business.

The more money and time saved, the more there is for the bottom line; and the more it can be invested into further business development or other key business activities.

To make a name for yourself, to excel in your market, and be a peak performer requires that you work smarter. Now is the time to apply a different business development model - one that attracts business endlessly.

Attracting business is the core focus of this chapter. A fundamental question you must constantly ask of yourself and your business is:

"How do we become more attractive?"

Answer this, then keep asking and answering it as you grow. The answers may surprise you, but they will lead you to growth and success.

9 Key Questions to Ask Yourself for Focussed and Successful Business Development

To become more attractive, you must first start by answering 9 key questions. Many businesses fail to address these questions and do so at their peril. Such businesses are destined to fail.

Be different. Answer these. Apply the answers. Receive the rewards.

1. Who do you need to be?

Perhaps a bizarre first question, but you attract who you are, rather than who you want to be. Therefore, you must understand who you need to be in order to achieve your objectives (and those of your clients).

You are what you think, and what you think about you will bring about. So to be a market-leader you must first think like a market-leader. For starters, you need to be proactive, understanding, creative, solution-focused ... You get the idea.

> *Action:* Write out the identity of who you need to be.

2. What do you need to do?

Knowing who you need to be allows you to then determine the necessary actions. These will be the actions you need to take in order to deliver your targets, goals and vision.

> *Action:* Write your action plan. (Please wait until the end of the chapter).

3. What are you looking to achieve by way of goals and targets?

In short, what are the key results you are aiming for that will determine the longevity of your business? If you do not know where you are headed, how will you know where you are on the way to those desired results?

Having goals and targets provides a way for you to measure your progress on your way to reaching them. This allows you to manage your progress more effectively because what is measured will be managed.

Action: Write your goals and interim targets.

Establish your key measurements to moni tor your progress. Be as specific as you can.

Post them up on a wall or whiteboard where you an constantly refer to them.

4. *What is your niche?*

If you have competition, you have not yet fully identified your niche.

By definition, a niche is your defined market and yours alone. No competitors. No price competition. Customers or clients make their decisions based on their need (that only you fully understand) and the value you offer.

Think of Cirque du Soleil. Their niche is so defined, that they operate in what is termed a "blue ocean" i.e. wide open where another competitor can't really operate in that space and as such, Cirque du Soleil own it. You could be the best and only business that offers your service on your block, in your district, or around the globe.

Action: Determine your niche. Narrow it down as much as possible until you can say you own it.

Share your newly defined niche with your clients, your market, and your network.

5. *What is the profile of our ideal client or customer?*

Considering your niche, this is perhaps the most unanswered and yet, critical question. Failure to address this question means you will likely waste time, energy, money and other resources due to a lack of focus. Perhaps you already have?

The power of answering this question is knowing the characteristics – even down to the fact they have 13.5 employees, an average of 2.3 kids, have a dog and are addicted to chocolate, send you 2 referrals a month, and always pay on time.

Please note - One crucial attribute that must be part of your profile is that your ideal client resonates with your values. When they do that you will have a long-term client. And that adds value to both sides.

When you achieve that level of detail, you and your business will be far more effective, efficient, and successful in attracting your ideal client. Start looking at your best clients and establish what qualities make them your best. Alternately, write out what you do not want in a client. For each point write the exact opposite. Sometimes clarity comes through contrast.

> *Action:* Write out the detailed profile of your ideal client.

Example: To get you started...

- Passionate about people development and has a training budget that invests >5% of the equivalent salary of each employee in their development.

- Has a great business network of >10,000 in database and a blackbook across many sectors throughout North America.

- Is a principle-centered leader and team player with great energy and experience as a C-level executive who has budgetary discretion up to $1 million.

6. *Where can you find your ideal client in the highest concentration?*

This is about knowing where the pool of hungry fish is so you can drop your "bait" (your product or service) into it and feed yourself for a lifetime.

First, your best and most valuable clients right now are likely among the ones you already have, rather than the ones you hope for. (This fact is mistakenly overlooked by many businesses suffering adverse consequences) They will likely abide within the top 20% of your clients – those who have contributed the most to your business. Continue to focus on them, as they are likely generating 80% of your current business. After all, it is often easier to do business with clients you already have before spending resources to seek new ones.

Second, put yourself in the mindset of your ideal client and ask this question again. (Where can you find your ideal client?) This client could be part of a social network forum, registrant from a blog, an attendee at an industry specific conference, or a social gathering.

>*Action:*   Do the research, identify the most likely
>   "ponds," and start "fishing."

7. *What are the needs of your ideal client?*

This is about putting yourself in their shoes and understanding their issues, challenges and needs. The ideal client wants you to truly understand them and their needs. They are not initially interested in hearing about all the wonders of your product or service. They want to know you truly understand them and their needs. Be interested before being interesting. You must know and address what is in it for them.

Do not leave this to chance. This may require investment of time, resources and research on your part. Your goal is to understand their "hot buttons". This will save you time, energy and money later on. For example, you could do a survey, review your testimonials, do some mystery shopping, run a focus group, desk research the industry, or just ask.

> *Action:*   Do your research and list the key features
> of your product or service. Match these to
> the benefits of your ideal clients or custom-
> ers.

8.   What makes you unique?

It is essential to establish what makes your product, your service, and your business unique. When you know this, it is easier to communicate and add to your attractiveness.

We often hear the term, USP or Unique Selling Proposition. It is far better to call it your "Unique Strategic Promise." The term, *proposition*, implies you may have some uncertainty whereas the term, *promise*, is a certainty – what your clients can expect categorically.

Saying things like, *our service or quality is what makes us unique*, is not specific enough. If your competition is saying more or less the same thing, you have not identified your uniqueness yet.

Appreciate that clients buy based on 3 things – service, quality and price. Unless you are Wal-Mart, you cannot offer the best quality with the best service for the lowest price. At best, you can deliver on 2 out of 3. Generally, your uniqueness will be about your quality and your service. However, you will need to dissect these to establish those key components that make you truly unique.

One simple way to determine what makes you unique is to ask your best clients. You might think you know, but they are the ones who have chosen your product. Determining your uniqueness can be done through a survey, reviewing their testimonials and/or consulting with them.

> *Action:*   Ask your team.
>
> Ask your best clients why they bought and
> what makes you and your business unique.
>
> Write out and post your USP everywhere
> – business cards, invoices, website etc.

9.   **What is your guarantee?**

The importance of a guarantee is often overlooked and yet is a simple, effective, and consistent means for you to add to your uniqueness in the marketplace. Without it, you will not really distinguish yourself from your competition. You are better than your competitors, aren't you?

Your guarantee must be deliverable 100% of the time. If you cannot deliver on it 100%, then do not guarantee it – yet. When you can, add it to your guarantee.

Note your guarantee needs to be specific. This is not your standard guarantee that comes along with your dishwasher or stereo. It needs to be really specific.

Sometimes a guarantee can become your USP. Think of FedEx – *Guaranteed delivery overnight or it's free*. Or Dominos Pizza – *Delivered hot and fresh in under 30 minutes or it's free*.

Note that as you grow and develop your business, your guarantee will possibly grow, as you become able to deliver 100% on more.

> *Action:*   Write out your guarantee and post it every
>   where and tell everyone.

Address these *9 Questions* and you will ensure that you attract, win, and work with your best clients. They will want to stay with you and they will bring others! The lifetime value of your clients will soar.

3 Strategies to Energize your Business Development

Your research, when addressing the *9 Questions*, will also give you good insight into what strategies may work best to help you ramp up your business development. Because the best focus is to attract ideal clients and new business opportunities, the strategies that will have the best effect are what are described as *Corn Strategies*. *Corn Strategies* operate from a place of abundance and understand the law of attraction. Consider the analogy of sowing corn. For each seed you sow in the best soil and care for diligently, you will generate ears of corn with more corn for sowing, and for your consumption and that of others; thus creating abundance. This perpetual provision will also allow you to take some "corn" and leave a trail that your clients will find tasty and will come back for more.

There are **3 Strategies** that are *great corn*. Applying these strategies, relevant to your business, will enable you to focus and to attract leads to you.

Strategy #1: What you need to be known for in your market.

Thought Leadership

When your niche knows you are an expert and you constantly and consistently prove it through the results your clients achieve with your business, which in itself, can be part of your USP.

Identify exactly what expertise from your skills, knowledge, and experience you desire to be known for by your clients, future clients and your network. Then craft some core themes within your field of expertise that you can expand on and communicate those clearly, creatively and constantly.

Ask yourself and your best current (or ideal) clients what venue of media they prefer as a means of communication. Determine which mode of communication will prove most attractive and provide you with the most credibility. Most people would agree that the internet is a key tool for this. Some potential media and routes include:

- Webinars
- Seminars
- Social media – LinkedIn, Twitter, Facebook

- Blogs – written, audio, or video
- You Tube videos
- Books
- Magazines & e-zines - publish articles
- Newsletters & e-letters
- Conferences – as a speaker, presenter, trainer
- Interviews – TV, radio, magazines
- Radio show – Blogtalk Radio

Depending on the media, take advantage of the opportunity to always present an aspect of your business. Until you have built a solid reputation, there is merit in offering your thought leadership for free. You need to plant in the minds of your target market the desire to know more about you and your business. To obtain the information, they have to contact you and/or make themselves available in your network. Then you can begin to sell more directly.

Action: Establish your area of thought leadership.

Identify media venues most suited to reach your ideal client.

Create your expert "messages."

Establish and implement your communication plan.

Strategy #2: What do you need to create that is resource efficient and effective?

Maximize Your Resources

This is about leveraging your resources such as time, money, competencies and other assets. A useful mantra comes from a quote from John Paul Getty.

> *"I'd rather have one percent of a hundred people's efforts
> than one hundred percent of my own."*

To begin to create leverage you must complete a self-audit and identify your business strengths and weaknesses. Then focus on harnessing and building on those strengths. You can address your weakness in two ways. 1. "Outsource" your weaknesses to someone else within your business for whom that is an area of strength. 2. Outsource to another business with that expertise. The amount of time and money you can save will be significant as it will allow you to focus on your strengths. This strategy will develop your business.

A question you <u>must</u> ask yourself every day is:

"How do I get more leverage?"

An effective and leveraged approach to reach your ideal client pool is through your network. Most business people know 200 people reasonably well, so at any one time you are only a step away from 40,000 people. So educate those 200 on your ideal client profile, your product or services, and what makes you unique. Give them some incentive such as a commission, contra-services, offer of an endorsement or a special offer to their clients. The more inspiration and detail you can give them, the more effectively they can work their own network for your business.

Most established and successful business owners will declare that word-of-mouth is the best way for them to grow their business. That may be, but there is one better - *referrals*.

When businesses talk about word-of-mouth, what they usually mean is that people pass them business over which often they have no control of the process initially. Having a referral strategy is far more effective when you, as a business, take control of all lead generation and proactively seek <u>*specific*</u> referrals through your network, especially your existing clients.

Another question to ask is:

> *"What other non-competitive complementary businesses also serve my target client?"*

The answer will provide you with other businesses to contact to seek an alliance. You can then provide reciprocal referrals. A couple of examples would be a real estate agent and a moving company or an accountant and a lawyer. Each pair of businesses would refer clients to each other.

The internet is a great tool for leverage. For example, you can use Skype for economical business calls, Ebay as a store front, and Google for research.

It is worth pointing out that *thought leadership* strategies are also *leverage strategies* because through one media you often maximize your connection with your ideal client.

Action:	Identify your strengths.
	Delegate or outsource your weaknesses.
	Document your network – who they are, what they do, how they can help.
	Establish your referral strategy. Be specific.

Strategy #3: What is the best long-term approach for your success?

Giving

At first this may seem a strange strategy; but when you give first, you will increase your attraction. Why? Because your focus is on the other person or business rather than on yourself. You are paying forward.

This strategy takes some getting used to because of its selfless approach. Giving is business by the *Golden Rule* – Do unto others as you would have them do unto you. For example, if you want to attract new business, give support and/or make connections to another business first seeking new business for themselves. This is like sowing corn. When you do so, you can expect corn to come up in greater abundance.

When your focus is on what you can give, what you desire (new business) arises directly or indirectly. By giving support to others, they will be more willing to give support to you. This is a very fast and effective approach to building the rapport that is a must for developing trust and long-term relationships.

What can you give?

The options are limited only by your imagination. For example, consider your assets:

- Your time - to mentor a not-for-profit business *pro bono* thus creating PR and a raving fan.

- Your money - to fund a university scholarship in your area of thought leadership creating a possible future employee.

- Your products and services - to a Chamber auction creating both PR and new business opportunities.

Note that when you are giving and helping and supporting others unreservedly, it works like any investment. Expect a return. You will become more attractive in the market and build value for yourself and your business.

> *Action:* Identify what "assets" you can give.
>
> Give strategically and generously.

The true power of these **3 Strategies** comes when they work synergistically. A great question to ask and answer is:

"How can I utilize all 3 Strategies?"

An example is to give a free webinar or seminar where you position yourself and your business as a thought-leader; this creates leverage through the use of your time and your network.

Summary

Exercise the *9 Questions* and *3 Strategies* and constantly re-address them. Your business will develop. Your performance will improve efficiently and effectively. Notably, you will attract and develop more business.

Address all the *Action* points and compile these into a practical action plan to which you can constantly refer and revise. The key word here is *action*. Your first action is to start giving. You will be glad you did!

Richard Norris has 20+ years experience from a progressive career - veterinarian, army officer, business and executive coach. From 23 years as a competitive swimmer has captained, coached and motivated sports teams and individuals to realise their potential.

Since 2003, he has focused on working with several hundred executives, business owners and leaders to grow their businesses and their people using a simple, practical and effective approach. As a result, Richard has won national, European and global coaching awards and presented and communicated at conferences and events across Europe and North America.

Currently, Richard is Head of Global Development for Lifestyle Architecture, the global people development company. His first book, Hoof it!, *is to be published in 2010.*

13 | **Buying Process Design**

Four Simple Steps that Make Sales and Loyal Customers

By Harlan Goerger

As a business owner, you know how vital sales are to the life of your business. No sales, no cash, no profit, and no business.

A simple view of sales falls into two categories:

1. A price and product focus that is generally price driven with low profit and high volume.
2. Value focused that is higher profit, lower volume and longer term driven.

There is a great disparity between these two approaches. The question is, "What do your customers really buy?" Is it the product/service or is it the outcome/results that your product/service provides?

Your answer puts you into either category 1 or 2.

The real difference between the two approaches clearly shows in the chart below:

To Produce the Same Profit without a Discount you need...

Discount	More Sales Needed	Product Handled
5%	14%	20%
8%	25%	36%
10%	35%	50%
12%	50%	74%
15%	70%	100%
20%	140%	200%

The question is, "How hard do you really want to work?" Do you want to handle 200% more product for the same profit as a competitor that is not discounting? How long will you want to continue working at this pace?

Decision time – if you choose category #1; you need not read this chapter ... it will not apply as your customers will not be loyal and you will have more staff turnover.

For those of you who choose category #2; please read on and absorb the information ... it will produce profits, loyal customers, and excited professional staff who will stay with you.

Warning – the following material requires effort, persistency, and continuous reinforcement; however, the rewards include higher profit, fewer problems, and a grander life style.

The Sales Language: Ok, here are all the magic words that will turn prospects into automated cash machines that hand over wads of money on demand!

Sorry, those words do not exist!

What does exist is a language salespeople need to understand and know how to use. The language is the customer's real needs/wants/outcomes/opportunities. This language generally has nothing to do with the product language. Salespeople that utilize this language connect with their customers in ways no product or price can! That means more sales, higher profits, and loyal customers.

Once you have this powerful language developed, it will become the keystone for the buying process covered later in the chapter.

A four-step process will help you and your staff develop the language for your product/service in little or no time. This process does require you to think like your customers, but shouldn't that be natural?

Step 1: Take a product/service and list all of the specific facts you can come up with. Facts are provable, not empty claims. "This is the greatest!" does not qualify. Examples include: it has an on/off switch, weights 23.5 pounds, and comes in 20 colors are all examples of facts. Place these in the first column.

Example:
A couch: has leather covering, has 3 cushions, and is a maroon color

Step 2: In a second column list as many benefits of a given fact as you can. Benefits are what the fact does. Leather covering gives these benefits: rich feel durability, easy cleaning, and cool feel.

Example:
A couch: has leather covering (fact)
= rich feel, durability, easy cleaning, and cool feel

Step 3: We now focus on the benefit and what the benefit really does for the customer. This is where our thinking has to change from product to outcomes. People buy cars not because they want a car; but because they want transportation that makes them feel a certain way. Insurance is purchased, not to have insurance, but to have security or a worry free night's sleep.

Example: Leather couch:

- What does a rich feel really do for the customer? How about an image of success, a feeling of great comfort, a feeling of achievement, a life style.

- Durability provides - A long-term investment, enjoyment time instead of upkeep, and a good value.

- Easy cleaning means - Minimal effort or work, an easy lifestyle, and alludes to a carefree home life.

A couch: Has leather covering (fact) = easy cleaning (benefit)
= carefree home life (outcome)

Are you seeing how the language in Step 3 really has nothing to do with the couch/product, but rather the outcome of ownership? If salespeople used outcome language, how would it be different than using product language? Connecting with customers would be one answer, plus we are talking high value rather than price so profits can be higher. I'll only pay so much for a couch (product), but what would you give to have a Carefree Home Life (outcome)?

Step 4: The 3rd step is often challenging enough; now for the highest paid skill in selling.

In discussions about selling or persuasion, the conflicting ideas of "pushing product/price" versus "leading customers to decisions" become the focus. Pushing product/price is going to cost you money, time and effort. Instead, we are going to focus on "leading customers to decisions" that are good for both parties.

To do this the salesperson needs to focus on "discovery or uncovering" the customer's true needs and wants. If I'm going to "tell you" all about my product, how do I "discover" any needs or wants? My mouth is open and my ears are closed!

Step 4 is creating effective "open" questions that help us "discover" what is important to the customer. By using our new results/outcome language as the starting point, we can create open questions that help us discover the customer's views, feelings and understanding about a particular result. By gathering this information, we can now fit in the product as a solution/opportunity for the customer. Which would you pay more for, a product or a solution?

To do this, take one result, such as "Carefree Home Life," and create open-ended questions with words such as "why, how, what":

- How might you describe the type of home life you would like for your family?

- What affects the quality of your home life the most?

- How might this couch fit into your home life?

Yes, these can be challenging questions to ask, much less create. But, think of the information and insight the answer will bring you! In one answer, you can gain more information than most "product pushers" ever find out.

Also, does this engage the customer in a higher-level conversation full of emotion, values, motives and images? Yes, we make choices based on emotion and justify with logic! It's the 50-year-old husband that just bought that expensive two-seater sports car and on the way home is panicking to justify it to his logical wife and young kids.

Create as many open-ended questions as you can. You will then be shown how to apply these with your customers and lead them to positive choices that are good for both of you. Yes, stop and do this now with your team.

Example: Couch

Specific Facts	Benefits	Outcomes	Open-ended Question
Leather covering, 23.5 pounds, maroon color, three cushions	Rich feel, durability, easy cleaning, and cool texture	Carefree home life; minimal effort or work; easy lifestyle	How might you describe the type of home life you would like for your family?

The Buying Process

Engagement

You are advertising and marketing to create a brand and awareness of the business and your products. This creates awareness only and takes up to seven impressions before the customer recalls you and your product. No, this does not "sell" the product for you; that is up to the sales staff when the customer walks in or calls.

A key point: In your advertising/marketing use the outcome/results language you have created and connect with your customers on their user level, not your product level!

Here comes the customer walking into your store and a staff member asks; "May I help you?"

"Just looking," states the customer (the expected reactionary response). No engagement or conversation here! Instead, the question, *"What brings you in today?"* will get you much further into the buying process. It causes the customer to think and engage with the salesperson.

Engagement is about observing, listening, and focusing on outcomes to engage the customer as quickly as possible. Old clichés like, "May I help you?" actually raise reactance – or resistance to being sold.

> *Home improvement customer: "What type of project brings you in today?"; "Tell me more about that?"*

> *Coat store: "What type of events or activities would you wear this coat to?"*

> *Auto dealer: "How would you describe your transportation needs?"*

These questions focus on the customer's situation, not the product. These questions gain insight while connecting to the customer. Three things are accomplished right up front with one question!

One way to create questions that are more meaningful is to take the open questions from Step 4 and modify them as engagement questions. You will have to experiment a bit until you find some very powerful questions that work consistently for you.

Just remember the Engagement step is about positively engaging the customer in a meaningful conversation about their needs/wants/outcomes/opportunities; thus moving you naturally to the next step of Discovery.

Discovery

The Engagement step gets the conversation rolling so the Discovery step can begin. The purpose here is to qualify the customer and gain enough understanding of their needs/wants/outcomes/opportunities to know if you can supply the answer; and their ability to buy that solution. This is called qualifying.

This really is the heart of the sale, yet "product pushers" will avoid this step and wonder why they always fight the price issue or worse yet, invest an hour with an unqualified suspect that cannot or will not buy anyway. Oops, the one that was qualified got tired of waiting and just left!

Take the questions from Step 4 Sales Language, and utilize those that fit for this customer. Listen carefully to what is said and probe more with simple follow-up questions such as:

- Tell me more?
- Why is that?
- How did that happen?
- Help me understand that better?

These uncover even more information and cause the customer to think more about their application/situation. Yes, many customers really have not thought through what they want and why. What value do you add by helping them do so?

Using open-ended questions, focusing on outcomes, causes this to occur in the customer's mind.

1. Visualize the outcome with emotion, ownership and logic.
2. Cause them to think about what outcome they really want.
3. Allow them to process the decision in their terms.
4. Give the salesperson the same picture the buyer has.

Because this causes the salesperson to focus on the customer and listen; trust is greater and the customer is more open to suggestion and direction. This reduces the reactive resistance that all buyers naturally have and moves the sale forward faster.

One caution ... do not short-cut this step. Often times a salesperson will hear something about the product, stop the questioning, launch into product pitching and just watch the customer shut down. Ask that next question and get the full picture! Customers want to talk about themselves and their situation. Let them and they will sell themselves. Yes, you can interject an occasional piece of relative product information when appropriate, but always get back to the questioning.

> **Key point:** *Psychologists have discovered it takes three to four questions to uncover true feelings and desires. This is the emotional part of buying. If you only ask one or two questions, you will miss the sweet spot and the most motivational aspect of the buyer. A little history lesson ... Socrates had this figured out in 450 BC.*

As you take the customer though this effective questioning, the customer will eventually say, *"How do I get this?"* Then help them get it! No, they do not need to know everything about the product; only enough to make their decision!

Most times, you will only need a few powerful open questions with a few follow-up questions and the sale is made!

Presenting Solutions

After a strong Discovery step, the salesperson should have a very clear idea of what will address the customer's needs/wants/outcomes/opportunities. If the customer requires additional information or a summary to make a decision, provide the solution in precise bits using (Selling Language) facts (step 1), related benefits (step 2) and tie these facts/benefits to the results sales language (step 3) you uncovered in the Discovery step.

Never add new ideas or information that is not relevant to the Discovery step discussion. This simply muddies the water and defeats the purpose of the Presentation step. The purpose is to summarize and solidify this is the right solution based on what has been discussed in the Discovery. We should only be filling in information gaps, addressing concerns raised in the discussion and reassuring the solution is correct.

How much information and pieces of product knowledge should we present? Only what is needed to carry the decision through to a conclusion. This might be one piece of information or several. It will vary with each person's decision process.

As to *concluding the sale* and obtaining the order, a simple decision question such as, "What are you willing to do to obtain this outcome? " will cause the customer to tell you where they stand. Keep the closing simple, yet action oriented. "As I see it, all that is left is the paper work, where do you want to start?" puts the action choice on the customer and causes them to continually move forward. All closing/agreement type questions focus on the discovered outcomes.

Comments such as, "Are you ready to buy?" are closed questions and can create resistance, pressure and a no sale.

Should *resistance or objections* come up, simply ask open questions about the customer's thoughts concerning the objection. Questions such as, "Tell me more?" or "Help me understand what you mean?" draw out the real thought process of the customer and continue the Discovery step. Trying to address objections with more product knowledge will create reactive resistance, which drives the customer away. Asking a question such as, "If that were not a concern, what would you be doing?" clarifies what the real issue is and isolates what to address.

The real issue is not to make the product the center of attention or discussion, keep the customer and their needs center stage.

Lost Art of Follow Up

The cost of gaining a new customer is said to be 4-5 times more than retaining a current customer. Yet, so many businesses concentrate solely on new business and seem to assume their current customers will stay forever.

In reality, a simple follow up plan can not only retain business, but build business with far less cost or effort compared to a new customer.

The key focus is "touching" the customer on a regular basis. This can be a note, card, phone call, sales call or other creative ideas. As long as the "touch" adds value for the customer, you create a stronger bond and future sales plus referrals.

A retail shoe clerk earns $80,000 a year selling $50 shoes. The secret is his follow up with all customers and how he services them. He gathers birthday dates for mom, dad and kids, anniversaries, wedding notices, etc. A card is sent to everyone, no matter how old or how much they purchase. He talks straight and honestly, often referring customers to competitors if the fit is better. The result, he has a waiting line of customers while other clerks stand around scratching their heads wondering how he does it!

What could you be doing to "touch" your customers on a regular basis and obtain this kind of loyalty?

Ideas such as newsletters, pertinent information, birthday/anniversary cards, special events, special offers just for existing customers, and thank you letters from your employees are all simple yet effective means of establishing and building loyalty.

The key is to have a consistent plan and execute that plan with each customer. A repeat customer costs you almost nothing compared to developing a new one.

Summary

1. Talk the language of the customer, not the product.

2. Effectively engage customers in relative conversations.

3. Question effectively with open questions that create images in the customer's mind.

4. Deal with resistance/objections through effective questioning.

5. Keep the focus on the customer's situation, not your product.

6. Create and consistently execute follow-up plans.

How to increase every sale: Many businesses miss some great opportunities every day. Customers are buying from them, laying out the cash, and the business has never trained their people to do one simple thing!

When people are buying, they are far more susceptible to suggestions or more buying. If the sales people/clerks would simply observe and ask questions, most sales could be increased at no additional cost! This works with large purchases or small ones. Convenience stores doing this see a 30% sales volume increase, which means more profit with less advertising!

We can up sell or add-on to sales though simple open questions that cause customers to consider additional purchases.

- "I see your family is here, how would travel games aid your trip? (Observe their situation; ask how an additional item would help)

- Did you know there is a real deal on (product/service) that goes well with (purchase), how might it fit for you? (Observe, recommend, ask how)

Anyone and everyone in your organization requires training in this skill set, even the service department. Imagine what would happen if everyone could add on to an existing sale!

Conclusion

It is your business and your money. Even if you have the greatest product/service in the world, it has no value until someone buys it. Training everyone in your business to understand communications through the buying process, the customer, and the power of open questions will set you apart from the competition and give you an edge that will have them scratching their heads wondering how you do it! It is up to you!

Harlan Goerger is *author of* The Selling Gap, Selling Strategies for the 21st Century. *With 30 years in the field consulting and training leaders in all types and sizes of business, Harlan has discovered what works and what does not. One difference that Harlan brings to his clients is the application of* Ethical Persuasion Science to Leadership and Sales. *He is President of H. Goerger & Associates, Inc. in Fargo, North Dakota and works with business leaders to improve the performance of their teams, key people and sales forces. He can be contacted at HHG@ HGoergerAssoc.com www.HGoergerAssoc.com www.TheSellingGap. com www.AskHG.com*

14 | Telephonic Selling

How to Be an 800-Pound Gorilla on the Phone

By Bill Guertin

Someday ... we'll have personal electronics implanted into our bodies for entertainment purposes.

Someday ... we'll have drugs that are engineered to turn off the tiny portion of our DNA that is responsible for diseases like Alzheimer's and lupus.

There will be a day when we will look at an SUV as a giant, hulking waste of resources, and a funny-looking, unnecessary relic of the past.

And yet, with all these changes ... people will still be calling other people to sell them something over the telephone.

Technology may change, our world may change, but the fact remains that proactive phone calls will continue to be a staple of our everyday lives. Selling via the telephone is – and will continue to be – a valuable, cost effective, and lucrative sales tool – especially in small business.

By understanding a few simple rules of success and applying them to your individual style, product, and situation, anyone can become a more successful seller using the telephone as their primary means of contact.

Step One: Do Your Homework

In selling any product or service today, it's important that you first understand at least a little bit about the person you're calling before you pick up the phone.

I managed radio station advertising salespeople for many years. Over time it became obvious which sales reps were destined to fail and others to succeed; those that did their homework before the actual sales call were far more successful than those that "shot from the hip." Today, I work with many different kinds of sales organizations to help them improve their sales results, and the highest-performing reps are those who take the time to learn a little about who they're calling BEFORE they make the call.

Being prepared doesn't mean that you should take an hour or more to research each cold call you make. Unless you're selling jet airplanes or skyscrapers, you need to engage in the kinds of quick information-gathering that takes a minimum amount of time and energy:

- **Look up the prospect's name on Google.** What do they do? What does their company do? Check their home page and any basic information that can help you frame your conversation. If you're calling an individual, you may learn what their hobbies are, where they volunteer, and any number of things that can come up in a conversation.

- **Check to see if they have any past history with the company**. If there's a way to look that up quickly, it may be worth a few moments to check and see.

- **If you're selling locally, check the local phone book.** Yes, people still print and use those things. What does their listing say about the kinds of clients they're looking for, and how can your product or service help them do what they do better?

Knowing something about your prospect allows you to begin a conversation more intelligently. As you'll see in Steps 2 and 3, it also allows you to separate yourself from the competition.

Step Two: Prepare for the Call

Once you've done your recon on the prospect, it's time to get yourself ready:

- **Know your goal for the call you're about to make.** What is it you want to happen as a result of this call? Do you want to close someone right away on your product or service? Perhaps arrange for a face-to-face meeting or appointment? Get an agreement for an in-home trial? Whatever it is, decide what will make the call a success before you dial. Writing it down on a call sheet or tally is even better.

- **Have any background information that you found in front of you.** Did you find out anything interesting about the prospect, online or otherwise? Have it at your fingertips, so that you might bring it up in conversation.

- **Have a short list of questions ready.** Don't rely on your memory or your quick wit! Jot down the 3-4 most important questions you'll want to ask in your conversation. (You'll see what kinds of specific questions you'll want to ask in Step Seven below.)

- **Remove all other distractions from your senses.** Mentally remove yourself from whatever else is going on around you. If you work out of your home, make sure the kids, the dog, the doorbell, the home phone, and other potential distractions are minimized.

Harvey Penick, the great golf instructor who trained many of the greatest names in professional golf for over 40 years, said his best piece of advice to any golfer, whether amateur or pro, was this: *Take Dead Aim*. Think of nothing else but hitting the very best shot you can at that moment, and take the time to look at exactly where you want to hit the ball. Harvey's advice can also be applied to telephone sales: Take Dead Aim with your prospect before you dial.

Step Three: Craft a Succinct, Honest Opening

Your prospect is bombarded with hundreds of sales messages every day. As a means of survival, they process these potential daily interruptions with an instant mental filter: *"Do I really want to spend any time with this opportunity?"* The split-second decision is made, and the prospect either ignores it and goes on with their day, or decides to process the opportunity further.

Your phone call will be treated in the same way as one of these potential daily distractions. Your challenge in telephone selling is to create enough interest in the mind of our prospect -- through the limited ability we have with our voice and our choice of words -- to cause our prospect to decide to spend a little more time with us.

The first several seconds of your phone call, therefore, is the only thing that your prospect has to work with to decide whether or not to continue to consider your opportunity. In just a few brief seconds, they're processing:

- Your tone of voice
- Your diction, including any accent or dialect you may have
- Your opening statement
- Your choice of words
- Your clarity
- Your potential competence in selling (as they perceive it)
- Your potential honesty and sincerity
- Your opportunity compared to all the other "stuff" they're dealing with at that moment in time

You have no way of knowing or controlling what events have taken place just moments before your call that has affected your prospect's state of mind when you call. You can, however, control all of the other things on the list.

Recent studies have indicated that up to 85% of our message is communicated in the way in which we deliver the words, and as little as 15% is communicated in the actual words we use. It doesn't mean that our words aren't important. What it suggests, however, is that our prospects are "reading" our tone, diction, clarity, and other intangibles and weighing them very heavily in their decision to spend any more time with us. You may be using the most successful, most highly-tested phone script in the world, but it's the way in which you deliver those words that will separate you from the others in your profession – and determine whether or not you'll get more than five seconds with your prospect.

So what are the actual words to use in an opening statement in telephone selling? There are a lot of options, but let's start by going over a few of the key things that your time-starved prospect will be listening for:

- **Something unique.** As a telephone selling pro, consider an approach that wouldn't be used by 99% of the sales reps that are calling on your same prospect. What would help your call stand out in a positive way?

- **Something sincere.** Authenticity has become the new currency of the successful salesperson.

- **Something beneficial to them.** There is no interest greater than self-interest, and so a realistic, pertinent benefit statement that hits the prospect where it matters most to them is very powerful.

- **Something new, free, or without obligation.** This is tricky to pull off in the first several seconds without sounding disingenuous, so I would recommend using this only if the other three somehow don't fit for you.

Here are a few examples you might consider. Remember, these words may not sound exactly like the words you'd use or the way in which you would phrase them; feel free to change the words around to sound like you, but be sure to keep the intent of the words intact.

Something Unique:

Hi, Paul, this is Bill Guertin. I'm a partner in a firm called The 800-Pound Gorilla; we create meetings and sales training that keep people inspired and on track to meet their sales goals."

"Hi, Paul, this is Bill Guertin from The 800-Pound Gorilla; we're the sales training company that helps sales professionals double their effectiveness in less time per day."

Something Sincere:

"Hi, Paul, this is Bill Guertin with The 800-Pound Gorilla. We create high-energy meetings to inspire employees, especially during a downsizing. I'm not sure if we can help you, but I wanted to reach out to see if it would make sense for us to work together."

"Hello, Paul, my name is Bill Guertin. We've not met, but I wanted to call to see if there's a fit for what we do. My company is called The 800-Pound Gorilla; we deliver unique, high-energy sales training that works for many different companies."

Something Beneficial to Them:

"Paul, it's Bill Guertin with The 800-Pound Gorilla. We help companies turn more of their cold calls into positive cash flow."

"Hello, Paul, my name is Bill Guertin. I saw your company's feature story in the last issue of Selling Power magazine, and I wanted to congratulate you for your positive press, and to share an idea I had for you as I was reading the article."

Something New, Free, or Without Obligation:

"Paul, this is Bill Guertin with The 800-Pound Gorilla. I'm calling

on behalf of the President of my company to invite you to be included in an exclusive Webinar for senior sales professionals on techniques to generate more business in today's cold-calling environment. The Webinar is a $395 value, but it's at no charge to you."

"Paul, my name is Bill Guertin, and I'm from the front office of The 800-Pound Gorilla. We help others to improve their sales success, and we have a new program that uses Webinar technology to give your salespeople the latest sales ideas with no travel expense. We're doing the first one for free, and we'd like to invite you and your sales team to join us at no charge."

Step Four: Gain Permission to Continue

It's a question that salespeople have debated for decades: Should you ask if it's a good time to talk, or just launch into their sales pitch?

My professional opinion is that there's not enough common courtesy in the world, and if I'm going to leave a positive first impression on a prospect – whether or not they buy today – I'm going to err on the side of being courteous. I suggest you do the same thing.

Here are a few ways you can ask permission to continue:

"Do you have a moment?

"Is this a good time to talk?"

"Did I catch you in the middle of something?"

"Did I catch you at a good time?" or *"Did I catch you at a bad time?"* (Some behavioral psychologists claim that by taking the negative stand – the "bad" time – you're encouraging a positive word from your prospect. The best one for you is the one you feel best about; it will show in your voice.)

Once you have permission, you now have a willing participant in the discussion instead of someone who's been dragged into a conversation without their consent.

Step Five: Prepare Fabulous Questions

Great selling involves an activity called active listening. Active listening includes the preparation of several excellent questions that start very broadly, and get more specific depending on the answers that are given.

By asking questions that lead us in one direction or another, we can gradually learn where the needs of the prospect lie, and whether or not there is a match between the prospect's needs and our solution.

I work with many sports teams to help train their ticket sales departments, so let's use an example of a Chicago White Sox sales rep selling season tickets to the upcoming Major League Baseball season. If a sales rep for the White Sox was to call someone in Chicago as a potential season ticket buyer that rep might begin to ask questions like these:

"Have you ever been to a White Sox game at U.S. Cellular Field before?"

"What was you experience like? Where did you sit?"

"Is that where you'd prefer to sit as a fan, or are there seats you'd like better?"

"How often do you attend games? How many do you plan on attending this year?"

"When you come to games, are they for business or for you personally?"

"Have you ever considered the advantages of being a Season Ticket holder with the White Sox before?"

"What considerations would be the most important for you? Would it be the seat locations? The number of games? The investment? Something else?"

"If we could find a program for you that fit all those criteria, would that be something you'd be comfortable with moving forward on?"

"Well, Mr. Prospect, based on what you've told me, here are a few recommendations I'd have for you..."

You'll see that we started very broadly (Have you ever been to the ballpark?) and then moved into the more specific questions about the prospect's likes and dislikes, their preferences, and their ability to say "Yes" if we were to find a match for them. We then let them know that we were customizing a solution just for them based on carefully listening to their answers and applying our knowledge of the product.

Every business and product will have a different set of questions, but you most certainly should have a similar roadmap to follow that will lead you and your prospect to determine what their best course of action should be.

Step Six: Know the Answers to Your Prospects' Most Common Objections

At some point, someone is going to have an objection to what you're selling. Maybe it's price, color, location, options, payment plans, or they just don't feel as though they need or want what you're selling.

This is where your preparation needs to be at its sharpest, because the reaction time you'll have to respond to your prospect's issues is minimal.

You must be ready with several logical, well-thought out answers to the most common objections you'll receive on the phone. If you know you're going to hear an objection like "It's not in the budget," take the time to craft several bullet-point reasons why your product or service's benefits can potentially overcome a budget problem. If it's "I already have a competitor's product," write out some of the benefits that your solution may have that are unique to your company, and why it may pay off to have your product instead.

Every company is different, and each company's products will have different responses from their potential customers. Figure out what the top objections are, write out the answers, and learn them cold.

Step Seven: Ask for the Order

It amazes me how often business professionals will answer an objection from a prospect with the talent and beauty of a graceful dancer, only to stop short of asking the prospect if he'd like to buy his product!

We cannot assume that our presentation alone will encourage the prospect to say "Yes." **We must officially ask them to buy.** We must actually use the words in order to realize the sale, such as:

"So, can we go ahead and put in the initial shipment?"

"How does that sound?"

"Shall we send it out to you this afternoon?"

"Do those terms look OK to you?"

"Let's go ahead, then, shall we?"

You should memorize several of these until they become as conversational to you as talking about the weather. Don't miss this critical piece of the puzzle! Unless we ask for the business, we as professional sales reps can't expect to get it – especially with something as challenging as telephone selling.

Step Eight: Repeat

Don't get too excited when you sell something, and don't get too upset if you don't. The very best in our field are even-keeled, and understand that it's a game of cycles and averages. There'll be hot days and cold days, and regardless of which one it is for you, the calls continually need to be made.

Remember that when people say no, they're not saying no to you; they're simply rejecting your offer. Resist the temptation to take it personally. Remember that even the very best telephone salesperson will not connect with every single prospect, but there are plenty of prospects out there that will indeed buy from you – IF you have the guts to tough it out and find them.

An 800-Pound Gorilla is a company or individual whose tactics and techniques result in an 'unfair share' of the available business in their category. You can be an 800-Pound Gorilla company like a Wal-Mart or a Procter & Gamble, or an 800-Pound Gorilla salesperson within a company or a business category; in either case, these are the ones who are next to impossible to compete with, and whose moves are watched and copied by nearly every competitor.

That's who I want YOU to be. The dominant player, the force to be reckoned with, the one that prospects think of first and fondest when your business category comes up. Follow these simple steps and apply them diligently, and you'll be well on your way to becoming that dominant player in your niche.

Bill Guertin *is a popular speaker, trainer, author, and Chief Enthusiasm Officer (CEO) of* The 800-Pound Gorilla, *a sales, marketing and communications company based in suburban Chicago, Illinois. In his own words, Bill "helps business owners and managers sleep at night." His speaking and consulting work is widely praised by business leaders nationwide for its creativity, energy, and authenticity. Bill warmly accepts new client and speaking inquiries at bill@The800PoundGorilla.com; you can find him at www.The800PoundGorilla.com, on Facebook, LinkedIn, and Twitter (twitter.com/800poundgorilla).*

15 | Negotiation

Stealth negotiating in Small Business

By Andy Miller

There you are, working long into the night on a deal that if you land, would bring in 75% of your quarterly goal. You are feeling pretty confident until, at the last minute, the prospect introduces a new player who starts playing hard ball and roughs you up. You are caught off guard but so close to wrapping up this deal you can taste it. So what do you do? Well if you are like most business owners and entrepreneurs, you negotiate back and forth and get the deal done. So now it's time for the bitter sweet. You won the deal but you had to give up more profits, terms, or something else of value and you feel a little frustrated, maybe even resentful. Now begins the slippery slope. How do you deliver what you promised but recoup a little of what you gave up? Does this sound familiar? Why do business professionals let this happen and better yet how can they prevent this common scenario from happening in the future?

Here is the challenge. Most small business owners do not have the time, ways or means to attend a week of professional negotiations training each year like professional buyers/lawyers do and do not exercise their negotiation muscle on a daily basis. Unfortunately, that is like taking a one day self defense course and then doing hand to hand combat against someone in the Special Forces. You're going to lose every time.

The problem is, what you have been told about negotiations is bunch of bunk. It focuses on the wrong end of the horse. Worse, there is little relevant information on negotiating designed for business owners and entrepreneurs. A few years ago a friend and I were attending a two day negotiations program taught by one of the world's leading authorities. The program triggered a major epiphany. Everything being taught in that two day event could be preempted before the negotiation process began. I turned to my buddy and said, "Look - 95% of negotiations can be preempted before the negotiation prep even begins!" He agreed and that was the beginning of what I call *Stealth Negotiations*.

Every book on negotiations will tell you about the techniques like: flinching, nibbling, cherry picking and the old "we are talking with a couple of companies." These books describe certain steps to negotiation preparation such as creating a list of what you want and then a list of concessions with an assigned dollar values to each. You need to make a list of their best alternatives if they don't do business with you and what you know and don't know. Then as part of your negotiation preparation you need to find the answers to your "don't know list." While these are all still good ideas, there is what something most people do not realize. By the time you begin preparation for negotiations, you have already lost! When you go looking for answers your prospects become aware that you are preparing for a negotiations battle with them so they withhold critical information. This puts you at a severe disadvantage. Now, unknowing of where you stand and if they have any real alternatives, you begin to feel vulnerable. When the negotiation begins you start from a position of weakness and are forced to make concessions, giving up much more than you should. The painful reality of all of this is that you were in a much stronger position than you realized!

I am going to reveal a contrarian way of negotiating. Something you will never read in a book or learn in a seminar. Are you ready to learn how to win the negotiation before it even begins? The key is to find out everything you need to know during the sales process. That means asking better, tougher questions and getting real. It requires an approach that I call "moment of truth" because if you do not discuss it and deal with it in the sales process you will pay for it later in the negotiation process.

Let's talk about some of the more common negotiation ploys and see how we can preempt these by asking relevant questions in the sales process. I am not saying these are not valid but why would your prospects spend their time, energy and resources if they aren't serious about working something out?

Some of the more obvious ploys are...

Higher Authority/Lower Authority
- I need to check with my boss
- I need to talk with the committee

Getting a better price
- Just had a budget cut so we need a better price
- We deserve a quantity discount
- That is more than we can afford

Getting more favorable terms
- Our cash flow is tight so our policy is to pay in 45 days not 30

Using time delays to invite incentives
- We decided to push this back to next quarter

Withholding communications
- They go silent, not returning phone calls or emails even though in the beginning they were very responsive

Using fear, uncertainty and doubt
- The flinch - you want what?
- Threaten to walk away or go with someone else
- Your competitor offered...

- We don't think you can handle the business
- We heard bad things about your company, service, product
- You're too small or too big

Before we look at where we can preempt these ploys in the sales process there is one other thing we need to discuss. Earlier I mentioned "the moment of truth" mentality. This is the moment when you need to listen to the voice of common sense inside your head and bring up for discussion anything that you feel would lead you into negotiations with the prospect in the first place.

For example the prospect says "Your competitor offered us a better price." Your common sense voice inside your head thinks, "That's odd, if they offered a better price then why are they talking with me? Why didn't they just go with the competitor?"

Now that you have that thought, let's bring it up for discussion with the prospect. You could actually say, "I'm a little confused. If they offered a better price then why are you talking with me?" At this point you and the prospect will have a discussion about price and what is going on. By the end of that discussion you will have more information on how to better serve the prospect and you know where you stand.

You have the concept so let's take a look on where we could have preempted some of the typical negotiation ploys in the sales process.

Typical Negotiation Ploy	Preempted in the Sales Process
Higher Authority / Lower Authority • I need to check with my boss • I need to talk with the committee	Preempted in a discussion about the decision process, how have they made decisions in the past, what title or functions are involved and who specifically?
Last minute change • Introduce new player at the last minute • Change the rules or understanding	Preempted in a discussion about the decision process and you verify they aren't going to introduce any changes or new players at the last minute. Then set expectations that if a new player is introduced or something changes last minute you would expect they will honor their word.
Getting a better price • Just had a budget cut so we need a better price • We deserve a quantity discount • That is more than we can afford	Preempted in the discussion about their requirements, time, efforts and resources. If they are willing to accept something different, what are they willing to invest, and the financial health of the company? Also, it is great time to ask them why they wouldn't get a better price from their current provider or your biggest competitor. Explore removing some of the bits and pieces they wanted to help get them a lower price and see if they can live with less. If they can't find out why.
Getting more favorable terms • Our cash flow is tight so our policy is to pay in 45 days not 30	Preempted in a discussion about terms and exploring other term options. Explore options that other clients have brought up in the past and see if any of those work.
Using time delays to invite incentives • We decided to push this back to next quarter	Preempted in the discussion about their time frame and why that time frame. Ask them why not push it back to next quarter and see if the time frame has an sense of urgency or impending event. Key: the party that has the deadline to meet is the one who makes the most concessions. Do you need to meet your quarterly numbers or do they have a real deadline?

Withholding communications • They go silent, not return-ing phone calls or emails even though in the beginning they were very responsive	Preempted in a discussion about time frame and decision process. Remember to bring up anything you typically hear as objections, delays, excuses or negotiation ploys.
Using fear, uncertainty and doubt • The flinch - you want what? • Threaten to walk away or go with someone else • Your competitor offered... • We don't think you can handle the business • We heard bad things about your company, service, product • You're too small or too big	Preempted in a discussion about requirements, competitors, fears and concerns. Good place to explore your strengths and your competitor's strengths to see if either of you has something unique the prospect can't live without.

Notice that I have brought up topics and issues that other peo-ple would tell you I am crazy for suggesting. They would say it is a high risk but I strongly disagree. Think about it, prospects are not stupid. Just because you do not discuss it with them does not mean they are not thinking about it and my experience says it is actually quite the opposite. I guarantee they are thinking about it so why not discuss it and find out where both parties stand. Having these conversations will help you both to explore and eliminate options. They are going to explore their options with or without you so why not be part of influencing their thought process.

Here is a case in point. I was on a sales call and as I was moving through my sales process with a prospective client, I asked what other companies they were considering for this consulting proj-ect. He informed me they were talking with a previous employee who was now a consultant, a well known company and me. I said the consultant sounded like an obvious choice, why not go with him? Next thing I know he is giving me all the reasons why the consultant can't do the job. Then I said the well known company had a great reputation. He came back and told me during his due diligence efforts he uncovered a lot of bad things that made him very nervous. Then I asked what he had heard about me and did he have any concerns? His comment was he talked to 5 of my clients (unbeknownst to me) and all had a great experience and were happy with their results.

Bottom line is through my willingness to explore his options openly in the sales process, he eliminated his options. I knew I was in a strong position and when it came to the negotiation phase he tried to tell me he was talking to other people. The funny thing is he didn't even realize he had openly told me he had eliminated the other options. I politely held my ground, made no concessions and got the business. I could only do this because I had asked all the tough questions in the sales process and preempted everything he wanted to use during negotiations. *That is stealth negotiations in action!*

Here is a little exercise so you can put this to work in your world. Download the *preempt negotiations worksheet* at www.andy-millerinternational.com. Now make a list of ploys and objections you get during the negotiation process and put those in the left column. In the right column identify where those ploys could be addressed in the sales process. Write down all the questions you typically ask but more importantly the ones you want to ask but for some reason in the past you haven't. Now practice using the moment of truth mentality and get real in your conversations. You will be pleasantly surprised on how easily those conversations will go.

Let's do a little review of the stealth negotiations process...

- Pinpoint the ploys and objections prospects use in the negotiations process

- Identify what questions can be asked during the sales process to prevent the negotiation ploys

- Ask those questions and bring issues up for discussion in the sales process

- Adapt the "moment of truth" and "let's get real" mentality

- You are actually negotiating every detail in the sales process so their negotiations posture is disarmed

- Focus on disqualifying them instead of qualifying

And here are the advantages of stealth negotiations ...

- Bringing up issues during the sales process creates a role reversal where the prospect sells you instead of arm wrestling in the negotiation phase

- Negotiations are over before they begin because you preempted all the issues

- If you do get to the negotiation phase you will negotiate from a position of strength and it is more of a formality

- It is the opposite of what everyone else does so nobody even realizes what is going on ... *stealth*!

I hope by now you realize the power in this approach. I have taught this attitude to thousands of business owners, entrepreneurs and sales professionals. When you preempt negotiations by addressing the issues in the sales process and adapt a moment of truth mentality you will enjoy the power of *stealth negotiations*!

Andy Miller is a 17-year sales strategist specializing in helping companies dominate their markets resulting in explosive growth by using his proprietary sales methodology. He is called "the best kept secret" by well-know business experts Jay Abraham, John Assaraf, Verne Harnish, Chet Holmes & Tony Robbins all of whom have used Andy to grow their businesses. Having trained over 18,000 salespeople, managers and business owners worldwide, Andy is a recognized authority on sales and member of the ASTD Advisory Board. He can be reached for consulting, training and keynote speeches at amiller@AndyMillerInternational.com or 703-822-8178.

16 | Virtual Presentations

Jumpstart Your Online Presentation Skills

By Roger Courville

As businesses look to improve their competitiveness in a soft economy, every method of reaching prospects and customers comes under scrutiny. Despite agreement that in-person communication remains the most influential way to market, sell, and train, often the costs outweigh the benefits.

Live, online presentations bridge that gap.

Online presentations in web-based seminars (i.e., "webinars") connect presenters and audiences from their desktops anywhere in the world in real time. But the opportunity of using this medium for communication brings with it an important question:

> *How do executives deliver powerful, engaging presentations to audiences not sitting directly in front of them?*

Why Webinars?

Webinars fill a unique place in the corporate communications mix. When considered in terms of time and place you have three options:

Same time, Same place (in person)	Upside: most effective Downside: most expensive Consider: If there is no concern for cost, you would have nothing but on-the-road sales and service pros making personal visits.
Different time, Different place (on-demand content)	Upside: reach Downside: least influential Consider: Written content, on demand videos, and any other form of on-demand content are indispensible, but if they had the flexibility and influence of the human touch, you would need NO sales and services pros.
Same time, Different place (telephone, webinars)	Upside: reach + human connection Downside: presenting online is new Consider: The telephone is familiar and powerful, but obviously lacks the synchronous visual connection to keep audiences "on the same page." Webinars go beyond just adding synchronous visual to a conference call with numerous new "surround" features to facilitate connecting, sharing, data gathering and reporting.

In a 2009 research study conducted by 1080 Group, 91% of respondents have attended a webinar, and they expected to be growing their own use of webinars by 148% in the following six months.

The survey also asked participants to rank a long list of potential benefits of webinars. A review of the responses of the most experienced webinar presenters found:

- Saves cost of travel
- Helps us reach audiences we would not otherwise reach
- Allows us to train more employees or customers

The takeaway is clear: webinars are no longer a novelty used by a few early adopters. For anyone who needs to reach an audience with a message, the trend likely changes the question from *"Should I present using webinars?"* to *"When I present using webinars, what am I going to do?"*

Before Your Webinar Presentation

Mistake #1: Not thinking, "adapt to the medium"

Scientists who study communication generally agree that the medium of communication affects how messages are delivered and received. You can tell a story in a book or a movie, and while each can deliver impact in its own way, we instinctively understand that the discipline of writing books and creating movies are distinct competencies.

Forty-nine percent of respondents in the survey indicated they spend more time preparing for in-person presentations than online presentations. Yet when asked to compare their preparedness for success, they rated "interacting in an engaging way" and "slide design" in webinars as the places where they're least prepared.

Simply, webinars take an audio-visual communication, your presentation, and change the way attendees engage with both the content and the presenter.

The first step in setting yourself apart from your competitors is to approach your webinar presentation as a unique medium, different from podcasts, conference calls, or a piece of video you create for YouTube.

Take Action

- Adopt a perspective of "adapting to a new communications environment"

- Invest in your own success by giving your online presentations due attention

Mistake #2: Not getting clear on what your audience will take action to achieve

Understandably a VFAQ (VERY frequently asked question) is "How do I get people to attend my webinars and pay attention?" Greater attendance often means more opportunity to impart the knowledge, skills, or calls to action that help you achieve your business objectives.

Invitees are most likely to attend – and be engaged – when they know the answer to "What's in it for me?" If you do not know what their motivations are, you will not be able to deliver messages that compel them to action.

> Case Study: Tapping into Motivation
>
> Client: Engine diagnostics client delivering training webinars to automotive technicians.
>
> Problem: Many techs don't know electrical diagnosis well, but should. Webinars covering basics were poorly attended. Direct surveys delivered inconclusive results in their discovery of how to message the webinars.
>
> Decision: Qualitative observation of *unspoken behavior* suggested that the content was valid, but technicians didn't want to admit they didn't know some foundational knowledge.
>
> Test: Added the word "advanced" to the webinar title and email subject line. Content of the webinar remained the same.
>
> Result: Quantitative improvement in registration and good post-webinar survey feedback indicating that the topic was, in fact, advanced in many areas for many technicians.

As the old adage goes, "people don't buy drills, they buy holes." Applied to your webinar, use built-in tools such as registration, polls, and post-event surveys to ask questions that go beyond "what?" to "why?" Understanding that direct questions may not elicit everything you want to know, plan to observe "unspoken" behavior as well (see above case study).

When asked to consider the content of online presentations from an audience's point of view, respondents sent a clear message with their top two success factors:

- "Clarity of the message and/or call to action in the presentation"

- "Invitation or registration page copy that accurately describes the content of the webinar"

If your hook is an educational presentation, do not succumb to the temptation to insert "about us/our company/our product."

Audiences will change the channel. This doesn't mean you can't deliver a direct presentation of benefits about your company, product, or services. Webinars are fabulous vehicles for reaching your audience with that message, too. But you'd be wise to set expectations appropriately.

Take Action

• Uncover your audience's motivations, both by asking directly and by observing unspoken behavior

• Prioritize the important and urgent problems or aspirations they are most likely to take action to solve or achieve

• Develop a clear proposition based on what your audience wants to hear

Mistake #3: Failing to hone the focus of your presentation

Presenters, especially subject matter experts, often suffer from "But But Syndrome," or the tendency to "squeeze it all in" with "but, but there's this other really cool thing you should know!" Research confirms that this is counter-productive.

Asked to identify what they find most annoying about a presenter's content, respondents' top concerns were:

• "Presenter tries to cover too much"

• "Presenter deviates from the message"

Influencing change only happens when presenters impart knowledge or skills that make it into the audience's long-term memory. The problem is that working (short-term) memory limits how much can be absorbed and remembered at a time.

Webinar software uniquely enables online presenters to listen and learn from their audience, honing that focus as the audience registers (answering questions) and participates (questions, chat, polls, mood indicators).

Take Action

- Ask, "If the audience only remembers a few key points, what should they be?"

- Cut out what does not clearly support those points

- Consider moving additional content into a handout

- Use webinar tools to sharpen your focus before, during, and after the event

Designing a Webinar Presentation Experience

Mistake #4: Not thinking visually to engage visually

The research of cognitive scientists supports two ideas:

1. Your audience will remember your key points more effectively if there is emotional impact.
2. There are verbal and visual channels by which they connect with your presentation, and your communication effectiveness *decreases* when audiences attempt to listen and read at the same time[1].

Since the webinar "environment" increases the importance of your presentation slides, you will optimize the impact of your presentation when you optimize its visual impact. Good visuals have the capability to induce emotion, tell a story, or illustrate a point.

1080 Group research suggests the same. When asked about

---

1   For a fabulous exposition of this problem and how to approach a solution add Cliff Atkinson's *Beyond Bullet Points* to your reading list.

slide design, the top success factor identified by respondents was "use of relevant images."

Thinking visually does not mean everything has to be a photograph, and you do not have to be a Photoshop wizard. For instance, a simple set of shapes created with the "shapes" function in your favorite presentation software may serve just fine.

The key is to have visuals to enhance, not distract from, the idea the slide is supporting you in communicating. Begin with visuals and then add words, not the other way around.

Take Action

*   Limit slides to one key idea each

*   Brainstorm possible images or graphics that would visually assist the audience's understanding of that idea

*   Use multiple slides to communicate a sequence of ideas. Don't lengthen your story, just use more slides

*   Favor visuals that are easily grasped, tell a story, and are persuasive

Mistake #5: Producing an online slideshow

In online presentations, the focal point of the audience shifts from you at the front of the room to their computer desktops. Improving the visual impact of your slides is radically important, but focusing only on great slides misses an opportunity to optimize your effectiveness though audience engagement.

Research in online learning suggests that experiential learning may be 15 times as effective as a lecture alone[2]. Not every presentation you deliver through a webinar is going to be a training presentation, but the principle is worth heeding:

---

2   Bersin, Josh. *The Blended Learning Book: Best Practices, Proven Methodologies, and Lessons Learned*. San Francisco: John Wiley & Sons, 2004.

An audience engaged with some type of interaction is more likely to retain your key messages.

Therefore, it is imperative when designing your webinar presentation to move beyond designing slides and design an experience.

Most presentations (with exceptions such as keynote speeches) have some form of presenter-audience engagement. Examples might include an opener like, "Give me a show of hands if you came from over 50 miles to get here today?" or taking a question when a hand goes up.

Webinar software includes tools that accommodate different styles of bringing an audience into the discussion. When approached intentionally, polls, Q&A, chat, hand-up indicators, and attention indicators enable online presenters to "keep an eye on," engage, and interact with their remote audiences.

Given the new presentation environment, it's imperative to design in your interactivity. Some activities, such as using a poll, may require setup. Others, such as a place you ask a "spontaneous" question, might slip your mind as your adrenaline flows in the heat of the moment. Plan for it.

Take Action

- Think through how you engage an audience when in person and map those activities to a new set of tools

- Identify changes to how you might interact

- A new medium also brings new opportunities not available in an offline presentation – identify the new opportunities

- Knowing that there is risk of multitasking, increase the frequency of interactivity online over what you would use face-to-face

Mapping Presentation Tools and Skills	
In Person	Live Webinar
Projector	Desktop sharing, web tours
Whiteboard	Annotation and drawing tools
Keeping an eye on your audience	Hand-up indicator, attentiveness or mood indicator, question manager
Audience feedback or group discussion	Audio: phone/VoIP
Written: Q&A, chat	
"Show of hands" from audience	Hand-up indicator, polls
Collaboration	Chat, Q&A, shared whiteboard, shared desktops, document/handout sharing
Handouts	Document sharing

Delivering Your Webinar Presentation

Mistake #6: Not presenting to people

Given how quickly attendees can multitask or worse, leave your webinar, it is just as critical to connect with them during a live webinar as during any other presentation.

When asked about their top annoyances with how online presentations are delivered, respondents overwhelming noted two things:

- "Presenter reads what is on the slides"
- "Presenter reads a script"

Their message is crystal clear: *"Talk WITH me."*

When presenting in person, we naturally look at our audience and occasionally glance at our notes. Online, however, we don't have the audience in front of us, perhaps increasing the likelihood of staring at the slide and reading what's on it. For some, the desire to deliver the perfect presentation or not forget something leads to using a script.

Just. Don't. Do. It.

The solution is to learn a new way to keep your eye on the audience. Like a pilot who learns to fly both by sight *and* by their instruments, successful online presenters learn to connect with their audiences by learning to use the feedback tools available in webinar solutions – and responding in real-time to cues from the audience.

There's an old adage in sales that "people buy from people," but it's not just a good idea for sales. Audiences develop trust and take action only when authentic value is being delivered. This doesn't mean you shouldn't improve your public speaking skills. Rather, you shouldn't waste their time in a live event being, essentially, a recording, or waste your time by not taking advantage of an opportunity to connect with them.

Take Action

- Value authenticity over perfection
- Make "eye contact" with the audience via the webinar tools

Mistake #7: Forgetting your "virtual body language"

Not every aural or visual cue you give your virtual audience can be designed into a slide or the overall experience. As you grow in skill as a webinar presenter, the next step is to excel at incorporating the virtual equivalent of body language, verbally and visually.

Most webinar software gives presenters some form of pointer, highlighter, or annotation. Leverage these tools to direct attention visually to the portion of your slide that you are speaking about.

A second skill to develop is delivering verbal direction such as,

"In the upper right portion of this slide you will see…" It is inevitable that a webinar participant will look away at some point in the presentation. Since people tend to respond to clear direction, and because they do not want to miss something relevant, delivering clear verbal direction improves your chance to recapture attention and improve your impact.

Remember that every presenter has his or her own style, and you will develop your own style based on your own strengths. Because most webinar solutions make it push-button easy to record both audio and visual elements of your presentation, you've got a built-in rehearsal partner.

Take Action

- Start with one annotation tool to direct attention visually. Grow into using others. Beware of overuse – you don't want to be a one trick pony

- Rehearse, record, and listen/watch yourself

The Bottom Line

Have you ever climbed into a vehicle new to you, reached to turn on the headlights, and the windshield wipers started flapping?

The problem with the task is not one of difficulty. It's an issue of familiarity.

Mastering the webinar presentation is the same.

The new reality is that webinars are opening up new possibilities. For some businesses they will be a way to present thought leadership and generate leads. Others will find webinars ideal for taking some appointments out of the sales cycle or improving relationships with their existing customers by improving frequency and reach of their communications. Most will find that the ability to synchronize visual communication to the conference calls already in use will deliver new and creative ways to engage and influence.

In the 1080 Group survey I've referred to, 74% of respondents noted their budgets have decreased or "stayed the same, but there is pressure to reduce." Given this, the rapid growth of using webinars, and the research suggesting this is a long-term trend, is not surprising. And this begs one question:

> *If organizations can increase their reach and increase their productivity by delivering effective live, online presentations, what will happen to the competitiveness of organizations that fail to adapt?*

Roger Courville *is author of* The Virtual Presenter's Handbook, *an internationally sought-after speaker and trainer, and Principal of 1080 Group, LLC. 1080 Group is a training and coaching firm helping executives design and deliver interactive webinar presentations and programs. The 1080 Group team has a collective experience that includes hundreds of clients, thousands of web seminars, and more than a million web seminar attendees.*

17 | Employee Engagement

Your X-Factor for Success

By Hillary Feder

"People are key differentiators in making companies more effective...the people development strategies go beyond pay..." - Journal of Organizational Excellence

Have you seen the Gallup Organization's latest report on employee engagement? For me, the data is clear: To be profitable, new approaches are required for leading and managing the people in your company. Gallup's 2009 survey estimates that 18% of the U.S. workforce is disengaged and another 53% are merely "getting by" in the work they do, resulting in a whopping $315-$516 billion in lost productivity. Disengaged employees underperform, become disenchanted, negatively influence those around them and eventually leave their employer. Engaged employees, on the other hand, are enthusiastic, contribute ideas, are retained longer and become valued ambassadors. The engaged employee will have a significant impact on the bottom line in any organization. What does an engaged employee look like, act like and sound like? Meet Ken, an engineer for a software company.

Ken's employer makes a habit of doing what it takes to ensure their employees are engaged. The company had been working on a new product for fifteen months and the deadline for product launch was quickly approaching. With much to accomplish in the way of product testing on different platforms and interface with other software, Ken was putting in long hours. Noticing that Ken was working hard to balance family commitments and work responsibilities, his manager reallocated portions of Ken's workload to other team members. As a result, Ken was able to be at the ball field with his wife to watch his son's soccer game. Launch day arrived and the project went off without a hitch. The VP of product development was well aware of the extraordinary efforts that Ken had invested to see this project through to completion. He made it a point to know Ken and what was important to him. After the launch, Ken was presented with a token of appreciation from the company. Ken was blown away. Why? Because the memento was incredibly personalized and demonstrated that his company knew him as a person. The recognition gift reflected Ken's interests as an engineer, auto enthusiast, volunteer, and most importantly to him, a father. The world has not always been this way. What's changed?

In the industrial age, physical assets such as machinery, facilities and raw materials could most often mark a company's success. Companies made "products" and people were a factor in production – viewed as "inputs." It was not uncommon to accept a position and 25 years later retire with the "gold watch." Successful businesses in the 21st century will look very different from those in previous generations. You might be thinking, "Boy, have things changed." Why?

Technology, globalization and people have fundamentally changed our world. Technology quickly becomes obsolete in the face of even newer technology. Competition is global -- ideas are quickly developed and can be copied almost as quickly as they were developed. People view their work as an extension of whom they are and expect the workplace to be a place for personal enhancement.

Technology has brought greater access to data which can be organized into information that can be easily transferable. Employees used to perform narrowly defined tasks in a simple framework.

Greater access to information has empowered people. Jobs that are not automated are not routine enough to be automated. The number of positions requiring interpersonal skills, technological and decision-making skills has increased. These positions require judgment, creativity, intuition, experience and empathy.

Globalization has changed the workforce. The pace of change is accelerating and has increased to a point where it is difficult to see what might be coming. Not all plans work the way they were intended. When they do not work, machines, capital, or strategy are not "the fix" -- people are.

People have changed the workforce ... diversity abounds. There are more women in the workforce. There are more ethnicities in the workforce which requires thought in communications, observance of holidays, and variety of dress and diet. The workforce is multi-generational with different expectations in the work setting, personality traits and values. In previous generations, people accepted unpleasant work and work environments for a good salary. This is not true anymore. People today expect their work to be interesting and challenging in addition to the growing opportunity for advancement. The younger working generation, are willing to make trade-offs between work-related status, financial compensation and personal lifestyle. In this paradigm shift, the ability to attract, retain and motivate people, companies need to reframe their thinking toward a more humanistic way of looking at their greatest asset.

The most-prized assets of a business have become the intangible assets that are not easily replicated: knowledge, reputation and talented people who are passionate and committed. People are transforming businesses. People want to be engaged in their work. What is engagement?

Engagement can be boiled down to the "X-Factor" – an employee is willing to give emotionally and intellectually to accomplish the work of the company. The "X-Factor" often takes them beyond their job description. The employee is passionate about the work they do and takes "ownership" for their contributions to the company. An invested workforce needs to be viewed as a universal need to all business environments. It is not industry specific or related to company size. Engagement is a simple concept, yet it can be difficult to execute. A devoted workforce takes time and patience to build, and must be cared for regularly. Unprotected, it can fade quickly. The results of an engaged workforce can be measured in greater financial performance, increased employee retention, and increased productivity. At the highest-level, engagement reaches the heart of your employees. Let's take a glimpse into how forward-thinking companies are engaging their employees.

Integrating a New Employee – Welcoming 101

A PR firm with 115 employees was concerned about the productivity of new hires. The question on the table … how can we drive productivity--faster? Many of you have started new jobs and can recall the first few days. It can be challenging to feel like part of the team. To understand the specifics, we needed to know first hand how new employees were being integrated into their new positions. A focus group of employees that had been hired in the last two years was put together. We asked them to think back to what they did and how it felt in their first days with the company. Here is a sampling of what we heard:

> *"I spent the morning in HR filling out paperwork."*

> *"My supervisor took me from HR to my new department. He didn't have anyplace to take me; my work space had not yet been assigned. "*

> *"My work space did not have a computer or phone extension and my supervisor really did not have anything for me to do or time to train me."*

And the list goes on. When asked how this made them feel we received comments such as: out of place, did they really need me, maybe I should have started next week. We shared the results with a cross section of company managers – the expression on their faces was priceless. They had no idea how these seemingly little glitches to getting a new employee settled could impact them in just this way. With information in-hand, we went to work to develop a practical, sustainable approach to welcome and integrate new employees more quickly. Plan in place, leadership at all levels received training on welcoming a new employee. Eighteen months later we formed a new focus group of employees that had been hired in the last year. Here is a little of what we heard:

> *"My supervisor introduced me to everyone in the department. At the next staff meeting I was asked to share a little about myself so that my colleagues could get to know me."*

> *"A few of the people I work with directly invited me to lunch and helped me learn the important ins and outs of our department."*

> *"The VP of our division introduced himself to me and gave me a portfolio and pen with the company logo – it made me feel less like 'the new kid on the block'."*

- A solid solution with a number of touch points that appealed to the head and the heart. -

Appreciation Can go a Long Way – Appreciation 101

A mortgage bank with 23 locations and 290 employees had mounting concerns about their employee appreciation program. This program had been built into their culture and had been important for years, but no longer seemed to provide the "lift" that it had in years past. The question on the table ... how do we get back the camaraderie and energy that this program used to provide?

Many of you work in companies that have programs embedded into the calendar designed to build camaraderie, a sense of community and goodwill. When an activity/program is initially designed, much thought and energy goes into the planning. Often in the first year or two of the program, there are many eyes watching for "how it's going." Once it is off the ground, a smoothly running activity/program is too often put on "auto pilot" with little energy used for taking its pulse or to understand what might need adjustment to keep it viable. To get started, we assembled a group of company leaders to talk about the program and how it was implemented. Armed with much information about what was currently being done to show appreciation to employees, we hit the streets and interviewed frontline employees through mid-level managers to gain insight. The comments were quite interesting:

> *"They are showing us appreciation by giving us stuff." Often the "stuff" is items from the company store with the company logo on it. We could just purchase these things if we really wanted them."*

> *"I really like getting gifts. The gifts they give us during employee appreciation don't really connect to the message of the company or say thank you to 'me'."*

> *"Sometimes I wish my manager would just outright say 'thank you' to me for some of these overwhelming tasks I am completing."*

After data collection, we examined how simple, yet important shifts could change the current paradigm so that those showing appreciation to the employees of the company could hit the mark once again. With a plan in place, training was developed for all levels of management from frontline managers to the CEO. Their new employee appreciation program looks like we have touched the hearts of their employees once again. Here are just a few of the comments we have heard since the new program was put into practice:

> *"I got a personal note from my manager talking about my contributions to the company. I didn't know how much she knew about what I did."*

> *"Fun stuff. I love the way it ties to the message our CEO keeps talking about."*

"Something with my name on it. How COOL that they did that for all of us."

These examples are snippets into the culture of companies that understand the value of employee engagement and are working hard to make this a critical business objective. It is important to understand that this does not happen in a vacuum and that engagement is a vital component of a company's success. So where does the responsibility start?

It starts with leadership from the CEO on down. Those who embrace this philosophy view employees as assets, not expenses. To deliver bottom line profit, these leaders understand the importance of building a dynamic culture that develops over time and permeates through the entire organization. They establish values for their company that demonstrate authentic concern for employee well being. They create an environment where work-life balance is welcomed and promoted. Engagement is deeply embedded into the philosophy of their leadership team and incorporated into the company culture. Leaders of an invested workforce have lenses that are focused and patient toward building long-term results vs. short-term quarter-to-quarter results. They have recognized the importance of having a direct connection to the pulse of company activities. They know that small and subtle shifts in how they think and react to everyday details can contribute exponentially to the big picture of what really matters in their company.

Leaders of engaged work environments lead and manage with key values top-of-mind. It is critical that your values are practiced by leadership and incorporated into how you hire, manage and measure. Company values printed in a frame that hang on your break room or conference room wall will not help your company build a culture or lead to greater employee engagement.

Eight values are necessary for every successful engagement system in any organization.

1. **Communication** – Leaders consistently practice clear, thoughtful, open and timely dialogue. It is imperative to develop trust that transfers among employees, across departments, and from the bottom of the organization to the top and back down again.

Encouraging ideas, listening and taking action is also a key component. Understanding that front-line employees often have unexpected contributions and great ideas about how do something better.

2. **Development** - Leaders who coach and develop their managers' "people management skills" can expect consistent implementation and execution of company systems. Through training and education, leaders cultivate opportunities for the entire workforce -- from new recruits to senior management. An environment is therefore created fostering and inspiring employees to master new positions and challenges. An atmosphere is built in which employees are able to learn and use a variety of skills to keep them and the company fresh. In this environment, employees readily reinvest with the company and it gives employees an opportunity to connect in ways that are different from their day-to-day tasks.

3. **Collaboration** – Leaders build teams. They recognize the benefits that come from collaboration: more innovation, improved quality, knowledge sharing and the elimination of silos in their company. Encourage collaboration among employees, departments and business units. Employees know that their opinions are valued and leaders understand the exponential results that are often the outcome of thoughtful collaboration. Collaboration helps build camaraderie and minimize the "us vs. them" state-of-mind. Collaborative efforts are a natural way to transfer knowledge and skills and groom a broader base of their talent pool.

4. **Autonomy** – Leaders foster autonomy. They have identified the importance of remaining nimble in their organization, especially as management structure flattens. Employees appreciate autonomy in the flow, pace and use of resources to accomplish their work. When employees are given the opportunity to participate in key decision-making it often reduces stress and creates trust and a culture in which they want to take ownership of challenges and take responsibility to finding solutions. They understand that the whole is greater than the sum of the parts.

5. **Authenticity** - Leaders demonstrate a sincere authentic interest in the well-being of their employees' lives and they understand the personal aspirations and state of mind. An environment that enriches their employees' lives by building a community based on shared experiences leads to work that has meaning and clear business objectives. It also engenders an understanding that thoughtful gestures and kind words speak volumes about their commitment and concern for their employees, which spreads through the entire company.

6. **Clarity** – Leaders bring a clear vision to the mission, to demonstrate commitment and inspire direction. Clarity leads to clear job descriptions where an employee has the opportunity to do what they do best each and every day. Jim Collins, author of *Good to Great and Built to Last*, explains that the right people are in the right seats on the bus. Employees understand the value of their role and how it fits into the big picture. When leaders are clear, employees are well informed and are able to manage their time and resources, and not get stuck "spinning their wheels."

7. **Trust** – Trust requires a leap of faith from leaders and employees. Strong emotional bonds are nurtured when leaders trust and support their employees and employees trust their manager. Leaders that are transparent with their vision of the company and its future will likely provide outcomes that are understandable and predictable for their employees. It should be a priority to share external messages first with employees rather than having them learn news second hand. When leaders instill trust within the organization, it is with faith that employees will act reliably and in the best interest of the company and its clients.

8. **Recognition** – Leaders who foster a well-integrated recognition system will satisfy their employees' basic need for achievement. Recognition sends a clear signal to an employee saying their work is meaningful and they make a difference to the company. Recognition which links specific business objectives to outcomes reinforces the organization's cultural values. Building accountability into the recognition system should

include measurements to monitor results compared to the original intention, then provide feedback. Program triggers should be reviewed and optimized continually.

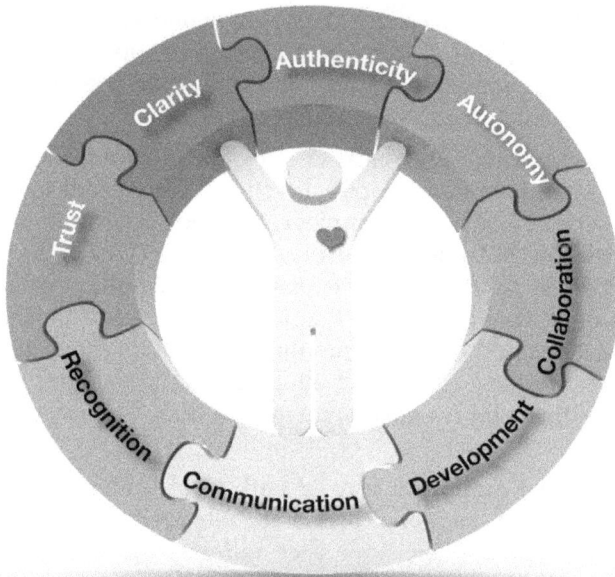

Key Values of an Engaged Culture

The long-term success of a company depends on its people. The reality is this mantra is easier to say than to put into practice on a consistent basis. The natural inclination in times of economic strife, when we are overwhelmed with downsizing and restructuring, is to only focus on the bottom-line. When budgets are scrutinized, money is scarce and the "soft-stuff" (i.e. non-monetary tokens of appreciation) is put on the back burner. In reality, incorporating the "soft stuff" of engagement is the solution to keeping up morale, building goodwill, resulting in positive financial performance.

Engagement is about appealing to the head and the heart of your employees. The key values of getting your workforce invested in your company are not difficult. However, it does take a commitment to integrate these values into part of your company culture.

Review and quantify current practices to benchmark where you are. Take steps to reach your employees where it counts, as people that you genuinely care about.

Successful work places will become adept at handling this new people-based economy. They will demonstrate the right balance of motivation and cost management. There will be work places that provide respect, trust, and a sense of belonging, autonomy and recognition. When people are happy in their work, they are productive and provide greater value to the organization, which ultimately leads to solid financial performance. Lao Tzu said, "The journey of 1,000 miles begins with a single step. If you are feeling overwhelmed today just take one step." Go ahead, just try it.

Hillary Feder is a leader in engagement marketing with a core belief that people transform business. Companies turn to Hillary for her keen understanding of how to get a key message to market that motivates, engages, recognizes or educates the intended audience. The results are strategic, innovative, creative, and results driven.

She is known for her collaborative style and strategic thinking. With a focus first on understanding "who" and "why" then "what," she uses a process to analyze a situation and develop solutions that are practical, creative, and focused for a specific set of parameters and change results.

18 | Invest in Yourself

To Build a Stronger Business You Must First Build a Stronger YOU

By Jeb Blount

Debbie was so tired that she was having a hard time staying focused. We'd scheduled dinner to spend time catching up on careers, politics, and the emerging trends in sales and marketing, but instead she was explaining how hard it was to find time for the things she needed to do for herself. It was easy to see how frustrated and stressed she was. As I listened to her plight, I couldn't help thinking about the many times I had heard the same complaint from other professionals. It is so easy to burn out and it often happens to us without notice, until of course, it is too late.

Debbie is driven. She gives tirelessly to her business, clients, and employees. She has achieved levels of success unexpected of someone her age. The problem she faced was, as she gave pieces of herself (her energy) to others, she was not scheduling time to replenish. Fortunately, she was aware that it was beginning to impact her well-being, peace of mind, and happiness. We discussed her situation and the options she had available for reading, relaxing, thinking, and exercising. She walked away from our discussion with one assignment: *she would schedule time on her calendar each day for herself and that appointment would not be broken.*

About six months later I checked in on her progress. Debbie's relaxed tone of voice told me all I needed to know. She explained how she was going to the gym or yoga classes daily and how she had almost caught up on her professional reading. I could hear her smiling on the phone as she proudly told me she had just been promoted to Senior Vice President. Despite the fact that she was given more responsibility with higher expectations, she said she had never felt better in her life.

She explained, "Learning to block out time on my calendar just for me is one of the best habits I've ever formed. It's funny how we will plan and schedule business meetings, sales calls, and client events, and then leave our most important appointment, time for investing in ourselves, to chance."

Small Business is Brutal

Running a small business is hard. The pressure to survive and the demand to perform is unrelenting. We must deliver results or we will fail. In small business, you are not judged by what you have done, but rather what you have done today!

Small business ownership is brutal and few can stand the pressure. The mental and physical toll on hard-working small business owners is unrelenting. Most people wouldn't last a minute in your shoes. Even for those rare and special people who thrive in the entrepreneurial environment, it is easy to burn out.

Little Pieces Of You

On a typical day, most small business owners get started in the wee hours of the morning. Many have to get their families ready for the day before they can even start thinking about sales work. You may even be a single parent juggling the responsibilities of parenthood and your business.

Once you get to the office, most of you start your day by putting our fires. It seems like everything is resting on your shoulders: you go on appointments, you make presentations, you tour facilities, you ask questions, you gather information, you give product demonstrations and showings, you endure conversations with your customers at lunches and dinners, you give proposals and you close deals. Each interaction takes a little piece of you.

Finally after a day of battle on the streets you come back to the office. You remove road blocks, deal with negative people and fix problems. You deal with back orders, employee problems, vendors, the bank and the government. Every problem, every road-block takes a little piece of you.

At the end of the day you go home to your personal responsibilities, i.e. your relationship with your spouse, your kids, your pets, your neighbors, managing the bills, the mortgage and a million other things. But, because you are an entrepreneur, your mind never stops. You think about the deals lost, the opportunities, the wins, the customers, and the roadblocks. Your energy is drained, your belief system deteriorates, and the stress takes a physical toll. As a business owner, the rewards are great, but if you don't put those pieces back, eventually you will burn out and you will fail!

Put Those Pieces Back!

The problem you face is that there is no one else to put those pieces back together again except you. So it is absolutely critical that you take steps to invest in yourself: *mind, body, and spirit*. You have to refill your heart and soul. Take time to focus on you. Take time to reenergize and build your positive attitude. Take care of your spirit and your mental well-being. You've got to take time everyday to read books about sales and motivation. You must make it a habit to turn off the radio while you are in your car and listen, instead, to motivational or spiritual programs. Exercise daily so that you stay in top physical condition. Eat and drink in moderation. Pay attention to what you are putting into your mouth. Get plenty of sleep.

Success in investing in yourself rests with your discipline to set time aside, written on your calendar, just for you. This appointment with yourself must be as sacred as a meeting with a top prospect, customer, or your child's piano recital. When you are strong and healthy you gain the Winning

Edge. You shrug off rejection. If you are knocked down you get up faster and still have the energy to fight back and win. Put those pieces back!

Invest in Your Mind

Ghandi said, "We should live as if we will die tomorrow and learn as if we will live forever." I've observed that people who continually exercise their intellect are happier, more motivated and invariably more successful than their peers. They invest their own money in seminars and workshops to keep their skills updated and sharp. They subscribe to weekly e-zines, trade magazines, and sales publications to stay current on the science of sales. They learn as if they will live forever and in doing so outpace their competitors. These business owners understand that by investing in the mind, they acquire the knowledge and skills required for accomplishment and success.

Read!

Everything you ever need to know about anything is contained in a book. Everything! If you want to learn something or become an expert at something all you have to do is read. Most of you want to be the very best in your profession. A key to becoming the best is to have more knowledge about what you do than anyone else.

There are thousands upon thousands of books and articles on the art and science of business. I'm positive that at least some of these books sit on your bookshelf but have never been read. Do you desire to read them? Sure, but you don't. It's not easy to find time to read when you have a business to run, a family, friends, and all of the obligations of life. The thing is, when you don't take time for professional reading, you quickly fall behind your competitors and ultimately give away your Winning Edge.

The problem for most of us is that we look at all of those books and get overwhelmed. We think to ourselves, "How in the world will I ever get to them all? It's just too much!" Then, because we are overwhelmed, we procrastinate. However, there is a strong correlation between reading and success. The secret to overcoming reading procrastination is to break reading into small doses. Just 15 to 30 minutes of professional reading daily will have an amazing impact on your life. Pick a time of day that makes sense for your schedule, block it out on your calendar, and keep this appointment with yourself.

Do The Math

Fifteen minutes a day of professional reading adds up fast. Most people who make a commitment to this practice are shocked at how many books they go through. When I speak to groups I'll often walk through the math just to make this point. Here's how it works:

There are 52 weeks in a year. Assuming that we only do our professional reading on week days, and that we take two weeks off for vacation, we are left with 250 days for professional reading. If we multiply 250 days by 15 minutes that gives us 3,750 minutes or roughly 62.5 hours of professional reading in a year. The average business, sales or personal development book requires about three hours to read. When we do the math (62.5/ 3) we determine that over the course of a year, when you read just fifteen minutes a day, you will read approximately 21 professional books.

This is an astounding number of books. At every *PowerPrinciples* seminar, without fail, someone will yell out, "I haven't read twenty-one books in my life!" Reading just fifteen minutes a day will change your life. Over the years it will add up to a college education many times over. Get started today. Grab a piece of paper and write down five books you will commit to reading this year.

Seminars and Speakers

There are experts on sales, business, and personal development who conduct seminars or who are speaking in every city. For most of us it seems impossible to take time out of our busy schedules to attend these events. The truth is, you can't afford not to go. Some of the brightest minds in business are speaking in your city today. They are speaking to civic groups, chamber groups or conducting stand alone seminars. Smart Sales Professionals and business leaders make it a point to hear at least one speaker or attend one seminar each quarter.

Drive Time

Drive time is an excellent time to invest in your mind. I realize drive time is also spent on the phone prospecting, maintaining relationships, and closing deals. Still, at a minimum, we have at least an hour a day of downtime riding in our cars. So why not spend that time listening to something good for you? The great Zig Ziglar calls this "Automobile University." Zig maintains that by just listening to educational and personal development audio programs in your car you can gain the equivalent of a university education.

I credit the hours and hours I have had listening to educational and motivational programs in my car with much of the success I've had. In my car I learned about setting goals, time management, the German language, and improved my attitude. I've "read" dozens of books in my car. In fact, this past summer I "read" the unabridged version of Emotional Intelligence while traveling in my car.

Technology has made it even easier to carry your books and motivational programs with you. With an iPOD, I can carry my entire audio library in my pocket. Now, when I'm on planes, trains and automobiles or have some downtime I can invest in my mind by simply pushing Play.

Invest In Your Body

What would change in your life, right now, if you began eating three healthy meals a day, dropped the junk food, and began exercising just 30 minutes every day? For many of you this step forward would change your life! You would feel better, look better and have more confidence. You would gain new energy that would propel you forward towards your goals.

The Strong Body - Strong Mind Connection

Business is often a mental game and your capacity for outwitting your competition is the winning edge. Thinking requires a tremendous amount of energy, especially in the stressful, emotional, roller coaster world of sales. Your mental energy is limited by your physical energy, so becoming physically fit naturally boosts mental energy. Major studies have proven that regular exercise improves creative thinking, mental clarity, and the capacity to bounce back from the inevitable setbacks you will face.

Stamina

A motto I've carried throughout my career is *"when it's time to go home, make one more call."* This means that when it's the end of the day, you are tired, and all you want to do is quit, you must will yourself to make one more call. I can tell you first hand that "one more call" has yielded some of my biggest sales. However, it's nearly impossible to garner the stamina to keep going when your body is weak and out of shape. You can't win if you lack the endurance to stay ahead of the pack during the long race to the finish line.

Many of you work long days running from airport to airport. Others are in and out of cars in the heat, rain, and cold. Most of you spend hours on the phone with customers and prospects. I know people who work so hard they have new soles put on their shoes every two or three months. How can you stay ahead of the competition, and perform, in this environment, if you are not in tip top shape? You need stamina in the tough world of sales. Just like an athlete you must be prepared to go the extra mile and break through the limits so that at the end of the day when your competitors pack up and go home, you make one more call.

Confidence

Face it, people judge you by your physical appearance. They want to do business with winners and winners look and feel confident. You know the feeling you get when you put on a new suit and look in the mirror? Your shoulders go up, your chin goes up and you instantly feel confident. When your body is in great shape that feeling is multiplied a hundred times. You exude confidence. Confidence wins deals. Confidence gets you bigger commission checks. Confidence is a defining trait of consistent winners.

Sweat 30 Minutes A Day

Being in great shape is critical for sustainable success yet, hard working business owners struggle to find time. How will you add a fitness routine to an already busy schedule? It is not as hard as you may think. The first step is to commit to 30 minutes of exercise a day. If you are really crunched for time you can even break your scheduled exercise into two 15 minute blocks.

The easiest forms of exercise are right in your own backyard. Take a walk or ride your bike when you get home at night. Supplement this with 50 sit-ups and 50 push-ups. On the weekends play sports or go for a hike. What if you walked and carried your bag on the golf course instead of riding in a cart?

I have a good friend whose motto is *"sweat 30 minutes a day, find a way."* For him, it doesn't matter what the activity is as long as it gets his heart rate up and sweat comes out of his body. There are literally hundreds of ways to build a 30-minute-a-day workout routine into your busy life. It doesn't matter what you do, it just matters that you do something that makes you sweat, for at least 30 minutes every day.

Rules For Food

Food is the central element in maintaining your health. In the hectic, driven world of small business it can be difficult to eat well. The good news, these days is that even fast food restaurants have healthy choices. With just a little discipline and planning you can easily find nutritious food on the road and you can certainly prepare healthy meals at home.

There are a couple of rules for eating that I live by. The first rule is moderation. I love food and some of the food I love is bad for me. I don't deprive myself, but I don't go overboard either. Enjoy your life and eat the things you like, but eat in moderation both in terms of what you eat and how much you eat.

One of the big problems with dieting is that dieting by its very nature violates the rule of moderation. Dieting takes us from one extreme, eating too much of the wrong foods, to the other extreme, eating too little of foods that don't satisfy us. When we get out of balance, it is more likely that we will swing back to our old habits fast and hard.

The second rule is that breakfast is mandatory. No matter what, eat something for breakfast, even if it is a cold piece of pizza. Breakfast is the most important meal of the day, it kick-starts your metabolism, energizes your attitude, and it helps you with the discipline to eat a healthy lunch.

Do The Math

Thirty minutes a day of exercise produces tremendous results. Even after we do the math you may have a hard time coming to grips with the shear number of calories you will burn. Take a look:

There are 52 weeks in a year. Assuming that we only exercise five days a week, and that we take two weeks off for vacation, we are left with 250 days for exercising. Walking briskly on a treadmill, you will conservatively burn 140 calories over 30 minutes of exercise. If we multiply 140 calories by 250 days we'll burn approximately 35,000 calories over the course of a year.

The secret to losing weight is this: *"Calories in" must be less than "Calories out."* It is as simple as that. Just eat and drink in moderation, exercise 30 minutes a day and you will lose weight and feel better about yourself. You will never need to diet again and at the same time you will stay in excellent condition.

Outlast Your Competitors

Over the years I've heard many wise people say that we never appreciate our good health until we no longer have it. Without your good health, you have little chance of leading a happy and fulfilled life. It will be difficult, if not impossible, to live your dreams and you certainly cannot be there for the people you love.

Running a business is physically and mentally demanding. The stress you endure is intense and unrelenting. You must be in peak condition to deliver peak performance and outlast your competitors.

Jeb Blount is a respected thought leader on sales and sales leadership. He is the bestselling author of four books, **People Follow You: The Real Secret to What Matters Most in Leadership***, People Buy You: The Real Secret to What Matters Most in Business, Sales Guy's 7 Rules for Outselling the Recession, and Power Principles. He is host of the popular Sales Guy podcast on the Quick and Dirty Tips network. His audio programs have been downloaded in excess of 5 million times. He publishes the weekly* Sales Gravy eMagazine *which is subscribed to by more than 200,000 sales professionals and sales leaders. In addition, he has written more than 100 articles on the sales profession. He is a regular guest lecturer for the University of Central Florida School of Business and a frequent speaker at the MIT Sales Conference. He provides coaching and mentorship for students participating in the National Collegiate Sales Competition and a judge at the International MBA Sales Competition sponsored by the MIT sales club. Learn more about Jeb at www. SalesGravy.com and www.PeopleFollowYou.com or contact him directly at jeb@salesgravy.com or 706-664-0810 x102.*

19 | Stress and Health Management

Keeping Yourself Mentally and Physically Healthy

By Dave Hubbard

A good friend of mine is a highly paid consultant to business owners internationally. His presentation consists of *Ten Absolute Essentials for Making Your Business Succeed*! The first, and most important of the ten? "Don't die!"

Most people live at a ridiculous pace today. The following poem says it all, and especially for the busy business owner...

> This is the age of the half-read page
> The quick hash with the mad dash,
> The plane hop with a brief stop,
> The lamp tan in a short span.
> And the brain strain, and the heart pain,
> And the cat naps until the spring snaps,
> And the fun's done!

For far too many business owners – lost in the hectic shuffle of spread sheets, and stressful heartbeats – the following simple truth is overlooked: The best way to manage stress, stay out of the hospital, and perform to your optimum potential; is to consistently eat smart and give your body the vigorous exercise it needs.

I learned that lesson the hard way. As a result, I now know firsthand the importance of staying in peak physical condition. For you see, I have had the unique privilege, and misfortune, of being both exceptionally fit, and seriously overstressed and unfit.

As a professional athlete in the National Football League, I was in phenomenal shape physically. I knew what it was like to feel great and function at peak performance levels. But when I moved out of the active world of professional football into a sedentary job and stopped being paid to exercise; my playing weight as an offensive tackle, combined with a serious back injury from a near fatal accident, made it difficult to maintain my health and fitness.

One day I was startled to read that the average life span of an ex-NFL athlete was only 53 years of age. I knew that if I did not change my lifestyle and take better care of my body, I would contribute to that statistic.

Through the agonizing process of losing my muscle and motivation to stay fit – believing that I had already exercised enough for several lifetimes – I found it virtually impossible to find the time to fit fitness into my busy life as a husband, father and business owner. However, after much trial and error, and having the advantage of many years of the best fitness training, I discovered the secret to getting and staying fit for life – *in only ten minutes a day*. Do I have your attention now?

The old saying goes, "You can lead a horse to water, but you can't make him drink." That's true, but you can salt his oats! It is my hope that the information in this chapter will challenge your thinking and change your life regarding how, and how often, you exercise; so that you can personally experience the difference it makes to the bottom line of your business. But before I get to the secret, it's important that you learn how your body works, either for you or against you, based on how and how often you exercise. My formula – successful now for over two decades – is as follows: Education + Motivation x Application = Results. Get any of those out of order and you will most likely fail.

The Most Important Part of Your Business

What is the most important thing in your business? Is it the computers, the patented gizmos you sell, or is it the machines that make them? The most important thing in your business, and the most expensive and sophisticated machine you own, is your body!

Since 1989 I have been helping busy business owners learn how to better manage their most valuable asset – their body! Far too many business owners today completely overlook the importance of properly maintaining the most important thing in their business – themselves. Here is the bottom line; if you are not functioning at full capacity; if you are not consistently performing at peak levels of efficiency; your business will suffer. And, if you die, your business will really suffer!

"The Body," wrote Theodore Herzl, "is a marvelous machine …a chemical laboratory, a powerhouse. Every movement, voluntary or involuntary, is full of secrets and marvels." Your body is made up of over 100 trillion cells. It has over 650 muscles, over 200 bones, and is covered with 4 million nerve endings with impulses traveling at 300 feet per second. Your body has over 60,000 miles of tubing just to carry the blood.

In one 24 hour period; your heart beats over 100,000 times; your blood travels 186 million miles; you breathe 23,000 times; your kidney filters 42 gallons of liquid; you speak over 25,000 words; and you exercise 7 million brain cells...at least on a good day.

Speaking of the brain; it is about the size of a softball, perched like a flower on top of the spinal column. It is connected by the finest fibers and filaments to every nook and cranny of your body. There are an estimated thirteen billion nerve cells inside the brain, and most of these cells have junction with five thousand other nearby nerve cells. Some fifty thousand of these synopses, or junctions, exist in your body, far exceeding the number of stars we know about in all the galaxies.

Dr. Daniel Anen, author of the bestselling book, "*Change Your Brain Change Your Life*," says, that as it pertains to your brain, exercise is literally the fountain of youth. Exercise consistently and you will change your brain. When you exercise, you think better, concentrate better, and your memory will be better. Exercise boosts blood flow to the brain. Exercise boosts growth factors in the brain that help you grow neurons! You say, "Wait a minute, I thought we were born with all the brain cells we would ever have." Well, here's some great news; ten years ago, scientists discovered that the brain can produce new neurons, and exercise makes it happen!

But wait, there's more! It is now known that exercise is the single best non-drug thing you can do to help depression. A head-to-head study compared Zoloft (considered one of the best antidepressants) with exercise. At the end of 12 weeks they were equally effective. At the end of 10 months, exercise blew past Zoloft!

Feeling depressed? Here is your choice: You can take Zoloft for 12 weeks and not be depressed – but keep in mind that 60-80% of those who use antidepressants suffer sexual side effects – or you can exercise for 12 weeks and not be depressed, have a healthier body with no sexual side effects. It's no contest!

A New Beginning

Do you know that every minute millions of new cells are made in your body? Whether you are 6, 16, or 65, your body replaces 300 billion cells every day. You replace about 1% of your cells every day. That means 1% of your body is brand-new today, and you will get another 1% tomorrow. Think of it as getting a whole new body every three months. With that in mind, it's as if you are walking around in a body that is brand-new since three months ago – new lungs, new muscles, new skin, etc.

The key to staying younger longer is to keep producing healthy cells. Whether your "new body" is functionally younger or older, whether it is functioning at 100% of its performance potential or at 45%, is a choice that you make by how well you take care of yourself physically! You choose whether those new cells come in stronger or weaker. Your cells don't care which choice you make, they just work with what you give them.

Eat more "real" God-made-food, full of enzymes and nutrients, and less "fake" man-made-food, full of preservatives and void of enzymes and nutrients, and you can change your body. You can restructure how you look, how you feel, how you think, how you age, and especially how you perform. It's not a miracle or a mystery. It's the biology that God gave you, and put you in charge of!

Exercise, and your cells get stronger; don't exercise, and they decay. When you exercise, your muscles release specific substances that travel throughout your bloodstream, telling your cells to grow. Sedentary muscles, on the other hand, let out a steady trickle of chemicals that whisper to every cell to decay, day after day after day.

Insidiously Sedentary

On average, we are seated for 12 to 16 hours a day! Living in the 21st century, one of the greatest obstacles to staying fit is that automation and technological conveniences have rendered most people sedentary. Statistics today show that 60% of Americans are sedentary, meaning they do not move unless they have to. About 30% are sporadic, meaning they exercise when they get a chance; but for most it is not often enough. That leaves only 10% of Americans that are physically fit!

Most people are not moving on a daily basis in the way our bodies were designed to move. Elevators, escalators, automobiles, golf carts, remote controls, gas fireplaces, etc. All these things make life easier but they are leaving our bodies behind.

I remember when I had to physically pull the garage door open, get in the car and back it out, and then get back out of the car and pull the garage door closed. Then when I got back in the car, to cool off, I had to crank a handle to roll down the window. Today I can do everything I just described by pushing two buttons! Though they may seem like little things, they all add up to sedentary living. As Evan Esar put it, "Walking isn't a lost art; one must, by some means, get to the garage."

This lack of movement is now forcing us to regiment exercise back into our lifestyle, or face the consequences of inactivity. Regular physical activity, that we used to get throughout the day by how hard our body had to work, quite naturally reduces the risk of developing or dying from some of the leading causes of illness and death.

Regular physical activity improves health by reducing the risk of heart disease; diabetes; high blood pressure; colon cancer; depression and anxiety; weight gain; and premature death. Exercise will help us to maintain healthy bones, muscles, and joints, and promotes psychological well-being.

The evidence is overwhelming. Increasing your physical activity will make a huge change in your ability to perform better at virtually everything you do.

But with all that said, why are so many people not giving their body the exercise it needs? Why do so many people tolerate functioning at less than 60% of their potential?

In Search of a Fitness Formula that Works

I have found that most people eventually recognize they are under performing and commit to some kind of exercise routine. However, they eventually give up because they either cannot maintain consistency, or they get frustrated by not realizing the results they expected.

Einstein defined insanity as doing the same thing over and over and expecting a different result. For many, exercise represents a similar kind of insanity. Exercise insanity is where you do the same thing over and over again expecting the same result but never get that result. This is where many people get stuck.

The type of exercise that best fits the above definition of exercise-insanity is aerobics. The following three facts explain where many people get stuck:

Fact 1: Most people do not know the difference between aerobic and anaerobic exercise, or understand the results of one versus the other.

Fact 2: Most people predominately do aerobic exercise, and the little anaerobic exercise they think they're doing is not really anaerobic at all.

Fact 3: Because of facts 1 and 2, people give up on exercise all together because they never experience the results they're hoping for.

Aerobic means *with air*! Aerobic exercise is a rhythmic movement of major muscle groups of the body, in such a way that you begin to breathe harder, taking in more oxygen (i.e. walking, jogging, cycling, etc.). The benefits of aerobic exercise are usually emphasized as cardiovascular and burning calories.

I strongly urge people not to make burning calories the goal of their exercise. Why? Because doing so can be very frustrating and confusing. You'll replace most of the calories you burn in a moderate aerobic workout by eating a bran muffin. If your goal is to lose weight and keep if off, you need to build muscle.

If aerobic means with air, then anaerobic means *without air*. I've discovered that there is a special group of people who understand the true meaning of anaerobic exercise, but are unaware of the fact they do. This group consists of any woman who has given birth. That is anaerobic exercise – and boy is it ever! During the birthing process, virtually every muscle is stressed. During this vigorous anaerobic workout, a woman can pass out because she's stressing her muscles so hard that she's not taking in much air. That is why Lamaze was created; to teach the art of breathing.

When I ask people if they are doing anaerobic exercise, I'll often get a response similar to this, "Oh yes, I now carry 3-pound weights when I walk or jog." Based on the above description I don't think I need to comment on how far off the mark that is.

Another misconception about anaerobic exercise is that it is strictly lifting weights. In reality, anaerobic exercise is any exercise done with high intensity, or the maximum effort required to build strength. This can be anything from lifting weights, to pedaling a bike, or running as fast as you can.

Here's the sixty-four thousand dollar question, what do you most want to accomplish with exercise? Do you want to (A) run a marathon some day, or (B) strengthen your heart and shape your body by building lean strong muscle? If you're answer is (B), it's quite possible you're doing the wrong type of exercise. If so, it won't be long before you're standing in front of a mirror examining your results, and the time you've spent doing so, and say, "That's it, I'm done, I'm wasting my time!"

The key to fitness is building strength to speed up your metabolism. Studies show that metabolism stays elevated for 15 hours after high-intensity strength training. Muscle is more metabolically active than fat. Add 3 pounds of muscle to your frame and you can figure in about an extra pound of fat burned each month, without even trying.

Besides eating smart, the key to dropping a suit size, rediscovering your waist, and losing fat; is adjusting your workouts so that you're doing primarily anaerobic exercise. In other words, short bursts with maximum effort. And, as science is now proving, that's also a superior formula for cardiovascular fitness, to build a strong heart.

This should come as great news for today's typical busy business owner, who barely has time to balance the books, let alone fit in a workout.

It's About Time

After repeatedly failing to be consistent with exercise by attempting to follow the standard recommendation of working out 2-3 times a week for 30-45 minutes; I realized the problem wasn't me, it was the recommended formula. Today, the recommendation is 30 minutes a day but it is not working! We know that it's not working because only 10% are fit! Something's clearly wrong with the recommendation.

As America's Fitness Coach, I feel my greatest contribution to fitness has been that I changed the paradigm. Rather than try to pound a square peg in a round hole, which is analogous to trying to force people into an exercise paradigm where most will fail, I decided to change the rules. If everyone's greatest enemy with exercise is time, and it is, why not increase the frequency, increase the intensity, and decrease the exercise time requirement to only ten minutes?

Here's my tagline: It's far better to brush your teeth for 2-3 minutes a day, than for 45 minutes 2-3 times a month!

To be successful at forming a lifelong habit, it is imperative that it becomes almost an unconscious part of your daily routine, just like brushing your teeth. Trust me, if you are struggling to fit fitness into your busy life, try the following and watch what happens.

1. **Exercise at very high intensity**: 80-100% maximum effort.
2. **Exercise on an empty stomach**: This allows your body to dig deep into its stored glycogen (stored carbohydrate) within the liver and muscle.
3. **Do primarily anaerobic exercise**: That is focus on exercises that maximize building strength.
4. **Exercise for a short duration**: 5-15 minutes (Long duration exercise actually enhances the production of Cortisol – the stress hormone. Many people are "over-exercising" which can dampen weight loss, energy levels, and immune function). This will play a key role in helping you to stay motivated with exercise as a habit in your life. Why? Because you'll see better results, while spending less time working out.

Finally, I draw an important distinction between exercise and a workout. Exercise is anything you do to get your body moving; take the stairs instead of the elevator; go for a walk whenever you get a chance; take every opportunity to play your favorite sport, golf, tennis, etc. In other words KEEP MOVING! A workout, on the other hand, is something all together different. Exercise can and should be fun, but a workout, if done with intensity, is not fun. That's because it's hard work! Your body was designed to be stressed, muscles, bones, heart, lungs, brain, etc.

Give your body the proper stress it needs on a daily basis and you will feel better, perform much better and have a much greater chance of keeping the first Absolute Essential for Making Your Business Succeed – don't die!

The best definition of a workout I have ever heard was from

George Allen, the great Washington Redskins coach. He said, "A workout is 25% perspiration and 75% inspiration." Stated another way, it is one part exertion and three parts self-discipline. Doing it is easy once you get started. A workout makes you better today than you were yesterday. It strengthens the body, relaxes the mind and toughens the spirit. When you work out regularly, your problems diminish and your confidence grows. A workout is a personal triumph over laziness and procrastination. It is the badge of a winner; the mark of an organized, goal-oriented person who has taken charge of his or her destiny. A workout is a wise use of time and an investment in excellence. It is a way of preparing for life's challenges and proving to yourself that you have what it takes to do what is necessary."

So put this book down and hop to it. If you start now, you are only three months away from getting a whole new body!

Former NFL player, **Dave Hubbard***, known today as America's Fitness Coach®, has been a fitness consultant to corporate America since 1989, helping busy business professionals take better care of their most valuable asset – their body. Dave was rewarded U.S. Patent for his unique ten minute exercise program in 1993. He has been featured many times on radio and television, and is a frequently published author on many major online health and fitness sites. His most recently published book is titled:* FAT to fit in Only 10 Minutes a Day. *For more about Dave go to AmericasFitnessCoach.com*

20 | Employee Development

Effectively Developing Employee Talent

By Tim Hagen

Employee development comes in many forms -- training workshops, seminars, DVD's and E-Learning just to name a few. The training industry's one major challenge is figuring out how to deliver truly successful training that is relevant and long lasting with a positive return on investment. Trainers focus on filling a room with students to educate with no regard to follow up or applicability to their students' issues. Companies send employees to public workshops or seminars only to wonder if their staff was able to apply the learning to their real world after the training was over. Small businesses cannot afford to wonder. With tight budgets, and a need for top-notch employees, small businesses must be getting the most they can from their training investments.

Small businesses typically do not have unlimited budgets for employee development, even though, it is critical to the livelihood of the company. An internal employee development program is a win-win scenario for both the small business owner and his or her employees. A successful program has three components:

1. Team Development

2. Self-Directed Learning

3. Coaching

The first component, team development, is to build teams that know one another and can work together. The second, self-directed learning, allows employee development to commence without expensive event based training. With the third component, coaching, the management team must be equipped to truly train and develop employees, for they are present daily and are best positioned to develop their workforce.

Team Development

Start by creating a "Team Mission Statement" such as: When we all work together and cooperatively engage for the betterment of the customer nothing else matters! The objective of a collective mission statement is to get your entire staff on the same page so that you can begin to build teams, and develop activities that keep employees engaged and learning from one another. This mission statement serves as the foundation of your employee development program. The following gives specific methods to begin developing your team.

Establish Relationships

Have your staff pair up in groups of two and find out three things about the other person they did not previously know. Each person will then introduce their partner(s) to the rest of the group. This is a simple activity that is effective both within and across departmental lines, as people get to know each other on a more personal level. This will open the doors to further communication, understanding, and helpfulness among your staff.

Build Commonality

Find another partner and discover one thing unique to their job and explain the value to the rest of the group. This helps to develop respect and deeper understanding among peers concerning their job responsibilities within the business. This exercise will deter negative or destructive assumptions that are often associated with a lack of understanding from other teams within the same company.

Build Awareness

Building awareness comes in two main areas. First, building positive awareness of one another's roles within the company and second, building awareness of tough issues. The key is to develop teams with solid foundational relationships and commonality — then they will be better prepared to confront and handle tough issues.

Building positive awareness of one another is imperative to building productive and happy employees. People need to know their teammates care and appreciate them. Team members should deliver positive feedback about one another. It's easy for people to complain, gossip or become negative about other team members; however, it is more important for teammates to reward and recognize each other. Building awareness also means developing the ability to confront and cope with such issues while NOT attacking your peers. Most employees will avoid confrontation because it is uncomfortable or difficult to do. Awareness of issues is imperative to companies working together effectively. The language of confronting issues is critical to engaging positive teamwork and interaction. When bringing up issues do so in the following positive ways:

"May I share an observation?"

"I wanted to make you aware."

"I wanted to share with you."

"We have an opportunity to (place issue here)."

Do not bring up issues using the following negative phrases:

"What you did wrong was ...."

"Why did you ...?"

"A dealer called and they are really angry with you because ...."

Address Issues Cooperatively

One's approach to giving or receiving feedback is critical to the success of any team. When giving or receiving feedback it is imperative that we consider all aspects of communication including our words, body language, facial expressions, and hand gestures, as all of them play a role in how we are perceived.

Self-Directed Learning

Training is one of those words that have numerous connotations associated with it; many of those connotations tend to be negative. When we first think of training, we often envision an instructor behind a podium imparting his wisdom to the crowd, assuming students will have the foresight to apply that wisdom in the real world. This style of training is time consuming, not real world applicable, and completely dependent on the quality of the trainer. This type of training is often thought of as an expense that is hard to quantify.

Training or learning does not have to take place in a classroom setting, and it does NOT have to be solely the instructor's responsibility. There is a way to reduce management time, decrease long-term training costs, and ultimately turn employees into high performers who, believe it or not, manage their own learning. You may be asking yourself, "How does this take place?" Actually, very simply, with a revolutionary concept called *Self-Directed Learning*. This extraordinary concept is taking the training and learning world by storm. Learning is the key word with this concept; it imposes ultimate responsibility of learning on the employee, instead of an instructor.

What exactly is *Self-Directed Learning*? It is a process that utilizes short lessons in 7 to 10-minute increments geared toward simulating the required skills of a specific job function. The activities are performed daily to encourage sustainable self-learning. Many organizations reward employees with point systems when achieving specific milestones. Once activities are completed, points are awarded to track the progress of each employee.

The major factor when developing a successful Self-Directed Learning program is using the proper techniques to achieve the desired outcomes. The following are the most common areas of training and how specific *Self-Directed Learning* techniques enable successful learning.

1. **Product Training** – An employee would be taught the basic elements or components of a product, and then the employee would teach it back. After all, it has been proven that to truly know something is to have the ability to teach it.

2. **Industry Knowledge** – An employee would be provided with reading materials on the industry with the ultimate expectation that they will either email a supervisor the information they learned or present the concept to management.

3. **Soft Skills** – Soft skills such as listening and presentation skills can be role-played by using specific scenarios that apply to the real world. To ensure the activity is completed, a third person could be asked to score the employees role-playing and have the score sheets turned into their manager.

4. **Positive Behavior** – Modeling is a technique in which an employee observes another employee who is assigned to demonstrate a desired positive behavior. The employee will then perform the modeled behavior. Lastly, the employee would email his or her manager and explain what was learned about himself or herself and what skills still need improvement, as a result of observing the desired behavior.

5. **Industry Workshops/Certifications** – If employees require specific certification and licensing at a public workshop they can leverage this event by emailing a description of three things they learned and/or teach their peers in small groups what they learned and how to apply the techniques to their jobs.

Designing a *Self-Directed Learning* program is a relatively straightforward process and any manager can learn the concepts and successfully apply the techniques. The key factor of a *Self-Directed Learning* program is matching the activities with desired outcomes. The learning activities must produce behaviors or practices that are desired from a results perspective. Costs of this type of program are minimal, whereas it requires only the time of the employee and their manager, without the cost of hiring an external consultant or purchasing material.

The following is an example of a *Self-Directed Learning* program for a sales person. Note the activities are designed with real world information and implementation of accountability.

Sample Cross-Selling Self-Directed Learning Matrix

Lesson	Link or Resources	Activity
Read Article on Cross-Selling	Sales and Marketing Management Article	Email your manager two things you learned from the article that you will apply to your everyday work.
Find a partner and apply one of the topics you learned from the article in a sample role-play	Sales and Marketing Management Article	Email your manager two things your partner did well and one area in which he or she could improve. The manager would then follow up and schedule lessons specific to the needed area of improvement.

Leverage the Real World	Real World Client	Email your manager a client you "successfully" cross-sold. Name two things you felt you did well and one thing you could have done better.
Leverage the Real World	Real World Client	Email your manager a client you struggled with in regard to cross selling.
Leverage the Real World	Real World Client	Email your manager a client you feel will be tough to cross-sell and set up a practice session with your manager. Present your concerns and ask to role-play the scenario out loud with your manager.

The key to a successful *Self-Directed Learning* program is to build activities that ask the employee to complete a task that includes everyday scenarios. When activities pertain directly to the employee's real world, management gains visibility to those issues, allowing them to address specific learning needs with additional training. The relevant lessons make a true impact on employees because they feel the activity is worthwhile as it helps them earn more money and obtain actual results.

The resources for a *Self-Directed Learning* program are literally endless. The days of only relying upon vendors and workbooks are gone. The resources that can be used for a Self-Directed Learning program are easy to find. The following is a brief list of resources that can be used when developing a *Self-Directed Learning* program:

- Salesresources.com
- Sellingpower.com
- YouTube.com
- Slideshare.net
- Salesprogress.com
- News from LinkedIn groups related to your industry

The benefits of a *Self-Directed Learning* program are equally valuable to employees and their management team. The following table presents these benefits:

Management	Employees
• They see the struggles employees have using minimal time investment. • They can make an impact on real world scenarios. • Staff is spending their time selling or providing customer service instead of attending all day workshops. • Once the program is set up, it is on autopilot, thus taking little time from management. • The methodology facilitates consistent learning and practice that cultivates skill development and eventual behavioral change.	• Employees do not have to sit in all- day workshops in which the content does not directly apply to them. • Employees deliver information to management whereby real world assistance occurs, thus resulting in actual success. • It's short and consistent (usually activities are completed daily with length between 7 and 10 minutes). • The activities draw upon real world scenarios. Employees will have immediate interest in the activity because it is not generic or hard to apply to their every day practices.

A *Self-Directed Learning* program provides many benefits to the small business owner including: improved morale, reduced employee turnover, less management time, and ultimately better performing employees. Once the program is developed, the materials and concepts are reusable. This is a great advantage for the small business owner for new hires and as the company grows. It is a great way to very simply allow your staff to learn outside of the classroom and still be able to reap the rewards of successful training.

Coaching

To coach staff to better performance some very basic activities need to take place. These activities are: finding out at what level their current performance lies, what motivates them, and then developing a performance plan to improve their skills.

The following diagram illustrates the basic steps of coaching.

Coaching & Evolution of Change

Level of Coaching

First, find out what staff members are doing well and in what areas they are not achieving their goals. It is critical to identify each person's strengths and weaknesses. Frequently, organizations tend to lump all of their staff together and train them as a group. Unfortunately, one staff member may be struggling with a skill-based issue and another may be struggling with a knowledge-based issue. In order to effectively train the group determine the key attributes your staff should possess and evaluate each member in those areas.

Second, find out what your employee hot buttons are. What motivates them ... is it bonuses, promotions, gift cards, praise, acknowledgement? Take that information and use it to design an incentive plan. You can get them to perform better by constantly fueling their motivation. Sometimes the easiest way to discover their motivators is to either create a simple survey or just ask.

Third, create a performance plan for employees specific to their learning needs and motivators. The plan should incorporate the attributes and tasks necessary for your identified reps. They will need competency in these areas in order to be star performers. How are they going to get to that star performer destination? They should have a specific targeted plan that addresses their individual challenges and recognizes them when they reach specific achievements. For one person a simple "Great job Bob on making that cold call," may be enough or maybe it's providing a gift card for coffee, both may go a long way to continue fueling their behavior. Management should have a good understanding of their role in the staff member's development plan and should remain active throughout the process.

Fourth, constantly check your sales team's performance through role-play, recorded calls, ride alongs, etc. Create deadlines for their performance improvement to make it easy for people to understand their accountability for their actions. Keep in mind that staff members will acquire skills and knowledge at different rates; so, be understanding and flexible when necessary with these deadlines.

Finally, REWARD and recognize appropriate behaviors and skills that team members have acquired -- it will go a long way!

Part of your job as a coach is to continually drive your team to desire a higher level of performance. If they have fun while improving, they will be more likely to do it. Come up with contests that reward those who come closest to reaching their goals. Always be prompt in telling people they are doing a good job. Coaching can take as little as 30 seconds a day, and if done correctly, will impact performance every day!

The key to developing employee talent in a small business is to leverage resources and build from within. If organizations position their teams to engage and work together along with self-directed learning and coaching, organizations can accelerate the development of their employee's performance.

Tim Hagen is the President of Sales Progress LLC, a sales consulting organization in Mequon, Wisconsin. Tim is author of the book, Quit Managing and Start Coaching, *and the architect of a revolutionary technology system, which utilizes the principles of Self-Directed Learning and Coaching. His company specializes in helping organizations set up personalized internal team building, self-directed learning, and coaching programs designed for continual and sustainable employee growth. He can be reached at (262) 240-1077 or by emailing him at Tim@SalesProgress.com*

21

Six Sigma

Are Lean or Six Sigma Right for My Business?

By Gary Gack

Perhaps you have seen an article that described how Jack Welsh used Six Sigma in General Electric to bring $8 billion to the bottom line. Or perhaps you have heard about the dramatic reductions in cycle time and waste achieved by using Lean methods in the Toyota Production System. Both of these methods of business process improvement have been around now for more than 20 years and have achieved dramatic results in a majority of larger firms and in many governmental units worldwide. Penetration in smaller organizations has been much more limited.

This chapter will describe how you can determine if these methods are adaptable to your situation. Our scope here is limited to what may be regarded as "core" elements of these methods; the various refinements and extensions applicable to manufacturing only are not discussed. I will describe how the key features of these proven methods can be adapted to smaller businesses and to smaller units within larger entities – an application of the Pareto Principle (the "80/20" rule). I will describe a "low-calorie" approach that will deliver a large part of the potential benefit of Lean and Six Sigma at a fraction of the usual cost. These methods can be scaled to fit – they are not just for the big guys!

As there are many misconceptions about what these methods actually are, I will begin with a straight-forward description of each method and then get into how you might go about deciding if they are appropriate for your organization.

What is "Six Sigma?"

In a general sense, Six Sigma is a *methodology* – a defined approach to improving any product or process. Six Sigma is also a *philosophy* that espouses "management by fact" rather than by opinion. Hence if fully understood and realized, it implies a significant culture change for many organizations. Opinion takes a back seat – "In God we trust, all others bring data."[1]

Technically the term "Six Sigma" refers to six "standard deviations"[2] from the mean of a set of numbers, which translates to 3.4 defects per million "opportunities" (whatever they are) - i.e., nearly perfect. This term often leads to a fundamental misconception – it does not mean we can or need to achieve that level of perfection in every instance. It simply means we strive to be as good as the customer and competitive realities require. Aircraft require Six Sigma (or better) quality - toothpicks do not. Many organizations use the Six Sigma method with great success and *never* actually measure "sigma level" – the stats geeks love it, but you really do not need it to improve business outcomes!

Six Sigma is concerned with reducing "defects"; defined very broadly to include any variation from customer's requirements. Too expensive or too slow may be a defect in the eyes of the customer. Six Sigma is also concerned with variation, not simply averages. In many business processes, the average may be appropriate to customer expectations. But if performance is excessively variable, a certain percentage of customers will be dissatisfied even when the average is sufficient. If we deliver in 24 hours on average, but 10% of the time it takes a week, then that may not be good enough in the eyes of the 10%.

---

1   W. Edwards Deming, *Competing on Analytics: The New Science of Winning.*

2   A statistical measure of variability and hence risk.

What is "Lean?"

Lean is primarily concerned with eliminating the "7 wastes" – *Partially done work; Extra features; Relearning; Handoffs; Task switching; Delays; Defects.* The primary tool of the Lean approach is "Value Stream Analysis" – a process mapping method that is used to identify and quantify the seven wastes. Various tools, most of them also used in Six Sigma, are used to find root causes of the wastes and to define "to-be" processes that eliminate or minimize wastes identified. Certain other aspects of Lean, such as work center design and total productive maintenance, are rarely used outside of manufacturing and are hence not part of the "core."

Lean Six Sigma ("LSS")

In practice, a "low calorie" Green Belt level of training appropriate to small and mid-size organizations incorporates elements of both Lean and Six Sigma without sharp differentiation between them. In the remainder of this chapter I refer to "Lean Six Sigma" (LSS) as a single topic. This approach is "lean" in the sense that it covers only the core, not less frequently used elements, and because it is delivered on the job in "just-in-time" mode over a period of several weeks or months – i.e., learn a little, do a little.

The core framework or "roadmap" is called "DMAIC" – Define, Measure, Analyze, Improve, Control – and may be briefly summarized as follows.

Phase	Key Activities & Tools (partial list)
Define	Identify a significant opportunity: create a "Project Charter" that defines the desired outcome(s), sets goals, identifies stakeholders, limit scope to ~ 3-4 months (don't try to boil the ocean) understand the current "baseline" process: understand the "Voice of the Customer" using interviewing and language skills to identify unstated and unmet needs, identify "delighters" process mapping, Value Stream Analysis
Measure	Identify and quantify factors driving outcomes ("Ys") using the framework Y=f(x), where outcomes ("dependent variables") are determined by the "x" factors ("independent variables") using brainstorming techniques such as Ishikawa (fishbone) diagrams; validate existing measures and/or gather new data
Analyze	Screen potential "x's" to identify the most influential using techniques such as correlation analysis, segmentation and stratification to focus on the "significant few"; when appropriate develop forecasting models using techniques such as regression analysis
Improve	Brainstorm process and/or product changes to drive significant influential factors (x's) to levels necessary to achieve target outcomes (Y's); prepare implementation and control plans
Control	Implement product and/or process changes; implement and monitor metrics necessary to ensure sustained performance at target levels; make the improvement "stick" long term

This process can be considered at three different levels of abstraction.

- Applying LSS concepts and principles informally – thinking quantitatively, managing by fact, using a systematic approach to improvement that does not 'fire' before aiming. An organization of any size can leverage this level.

- "Low calorie" LSS using part-time LSS practitioners (Green Belts) who are formally trained in the core principles and may be "certified" based on actual project performance rather than by taking a test – results trump traditional certification. This level is generally applicable to firms in the 20 – 500 employee range.

- "Traditional" LSS programs that add formally trained and certified full time specialists called "Black Belts". This level becomes feasible and useful at somewhere around 500 or more employees.

Do We Need LSS?

The answer to that question really depends on where you stand relative to your competition and customer's expectations. If you are "king of the hill" in terms of customer service, cost structure, market share, quality, and any other factors significant to your success, then the answer is a resounding, "NO!"

If you are not lord of all you survey, if you have significant results gaps relative to competitors and customer expectations, then the answer may well be, "YES!" LSS is very effective in closing gaps between current performance and "best in class" benchmarks. LSS is about dramatic step change improvement – if you are satisfied with 5% improvement, you do not need these high-powered tools.

In some cases these methods will be used to solve a problem you are painfully aware of. Perhaps your costs are too high, or your cycle times are too long. You know what the problem is, but perhaps you do not know what actions to take to achieve a long-term fix. On the other hand, you may not know exactly what the problem is. You may be losing market share but are not sure of the reason why. The Six Sigma DMAIC framework can be used to address both classes of problems; to fix what you know is a problem, or to discover the root cause of a symptom that is not well understood.

Can We Afford It?

To be frank, if you follow the "traditional" approach used by many large multi-nationals, the answer is *probably not.* As classically defined and implemented, a Six Sigma program trains a cadre of process improvement specialists known as "belts" of various hues. "Black Belts" typically receive 4 weeks of training and are in most instances, dedicated full time to process improvement.

Companies like GE and Motorola train thousands of these, and generally expected each one to deliver $1,000,000 - $2,000,000 in net benefits per year. In addition, most of the big guys train additional thousands of "Green Belts" – usually providing 1 or 2 weeks of training. They may expect these individuals to devote perhaps 20% of their time to process improvement projects and to deliver $50,000 - $200,000 in net benefit per project. Others, called "Yellow Belts," have a day or two of orientation and work in improvement teams on a very part time basis, under supervision of Green and/or Black Belts. All of that makes sense if you have tens or hundreds of thousands of employees, but clearly does not if you are much smaller.

More recently some training providers have devised "low calorie" training designed to deliver the core "Green Belt" level ideas in a few days – the key 80% at a fraction of the traditional cost. Excellent Green Belt programs are available as eLearning for single individuals at around $500 per person. This level of training is sufficient for most of the typical problems encountered in small to mid-size organizations. In general, a Green Belt will be able to deliver substantial net benefits by devoting perhaps one day per week to process improvement projects.

There are many reasons the number of persons you might

assign can vary, but a rough "rule of thumb" suggests training a number of Green Belts equivalent to about 1% of total staff hours. If you have 20 people in your organization, that equates to one person devoted to LSS projects which is 20% of their time. In addition to the cost of training, it is likely you both will need a bit of consulting/coaching advice from an experienced Lean/Six Sigma professional. You can expect to pay rates similar to those you pay your attorney or CPA – generally in the range of $150 - $250 per hour. In a typical situation, each Green Belt might need four to eight hours of coaching over a period of several months to help them get started. *The amount of consulting help needed may vary as a function of the experience and capability of those you select to train.*

Let's look at several typical cost/benefit scenarios scaled to different size organizations. For this illustration I make various assumptions that I find from experience are generally reasonable for many firms. Some of these assumptions, such as staff compensation, are subject to significant variation. Benefits projections assume the per project benefit likely to be realized increases with organization size; simply because improvement opportunity and size generally grow in sync. For those who may be interested, I will be happy to provide an Excel spreadsheet you can use to "what if" for your own assumptions.

Return on investment estimates given here are conservative relative to experience in larger organizations where ROI is generally reported in the 3-10x range. For simplicity, I have assumed you would train the numbers of individuals indicated all at once, but of course in reality, it is likely the training would be staggered.

Total Headcount	< 20	20	40	100	500
Apply Principles informally	X	X	X	X	X
Trained & Certified Green Belts	-	1@20%	2@20%	5@20%	20@20%
Trained & Certified Black Belts	-	-	-	-	1@100%
Year 1 Cost	?	$21,300	$42,600	$106,500	$660,000
Year 1 Net Benefit	?	$50,000	$140,000	$500,000	$2,450,000
Year 1 ROI	?	2.3	3.3	4.7	3.7
Year 1 Costs		**$21,300**	**$42,600**	**$106,500**	**$660,000**
Green Belt Salary @ $100k loaded		$20,000	$40,000	$100,000	$500,000
Black Belt Salary @ $150k loaded					$150,000
Training (eLearning)		$500	$1,000	$2,500	$10,000
Coaching @ $200/hour		$800	$1,600	$2,500	$10,000
Year 1 Net Benefits		**$50,000**	**$140,000**	**$500,000**	**$2,450,000**
Net $ Savings per GB project		$25,000	$35,000	$50,000	$50,000
# GB Projects Completed		2	4	10	40
Net $ Savings per BB project					$150,000
# BB project completed					3

I recommend you develop a model like this with values appropriate to your organization. If the indicated ROI numbers look attractive to you relative to other opportunities that may be available, it makes sense to think seriously about moving forward.

Critical Success Factors

First and foremost is the style and attitude of the executive team, especially the owner or CEO. Certainly there are many successful organizations that operate in fire-ready-aim mode. If you are one of those, and that style is working for you, LSS is probably going to go against your grain. No point swimming against the tide – if it is not your style, so be it. If on the other hand, you prefer to think things through carefully and you have a preference for facts and data, LSS may be a good fit.

Assuming LSS is consistent with your style, the next most critical factor is project selection. Focus on the things most important to your success – things like win (or loss) percentages, warranty costs, defects and rework, or customer satisfaction. Do a somewhat formal organizational assessment. What are your strengths and weaknesses? What threats or opportunities do you face? Rank them. Evaluate where you are relative to "best in class" in each important area. When there are significant gaps between your current performance and best in class, those are excellent areas to initiate DMAIC projects. Set aggressive goals, recognizing they may or may not be achievable. Adjust goals later if it makes sense to do so. Seek to close at least 50% of the gap relative to best in class. Five percent improvements are for sissies. Swing for the fence!

Next, think through whom in your team makes a good Green Belt candidate. The ones you want are the ones who probably already have too much to do; the rising stars. Sending someone to training because they happen to be available or are charming dinner companions is usually not a formula for success. People already accustomed to quantitative thinking are often good candidates, provided they are able to see the big picture. Some engineers or accountants may be good candidates if they are able to distinguish forest from trees. Statistical knowledge can be helpful, but is not essential.

Each project needs an executive sponsor willing to devote time and attention to the project. The sponsor, often jointly with the assigned Green Belt, will prepare and as necessary, adjust a Project Charter. Most importantly, the sponsor ensures the Green Belt's responsibilities are off-loaded sufficiently to ensure an adequate amount of time is actually devoted to the selected project. The sponsor helps and guides the Green Belt by removing roadblocks, ensuring necessary resources and access, and conducting "tollgate reviews" at the end of each phase to ensure the project is progressing satisfactorily. The sponsor enforces MBA rule 1 – "ignore sunk cost." If it becomes clear at any tollgate review that the project is unlikely to succeed it is the sponsor's job to cancel the project. Don't throw good money after bad.

Possible Next Steps

The considerations raised in this chapter might make a great agenda for your next leadership team meeting or off-site. Thinking through your strategic position and evaluating your strengths and weakness can be a very valuable exercise, whether or not you conclude Lean Six Sigma is a fit.

Gary Gack, is the founder and President of Process-Fusion.net, a provider of e-Learning, assessments, strategy advice, training, and coaching relating to integration and deployment of best practices. Mr. Gack holds an MBA from the Wharton School and is a Lean Six Sigma Black Belt. He has more than 40 years of diverse experience, including more than 20 years focused on process improvement. He is the author of many articles and a book entitled Managing the "Black Hole: The Executive's Guide to Software Project Risk.

22 | Sarbanes-Oxley & Compliance

Leveraging Best Practices to Combat Fraud

Peg Jackson, DPA, CPCU

Which one of these people would be most likely to embezzle or misappropriate your company's funds or assets?

a. A single mother, aged 23, whose home is about to go into foreclosure.
b. A recent immigrant who works part-time during the evenings in your warehouse.
c. A middle-aged man, who is a college graduate, owns his own home and has children in college.

If you answered "c," you are correct. Contrary to popular belief, employees who are more likely to misappropriate company funds or assets tend to be middle-age men who are college educated. The primary factors that facilitate fraud in small businesses are 1) a work environment that lacks controls and oversight, 2) the reluctance of co-workers to report fraud and 3) failure to implement SOX Best Practices.

The best practices that emerged from Sarbanes-Oxley legislation presents value and opportunity for small businesses in creating sustainable infrastructures, reducing fraud and improving the company's bottom line. SOX compliance and best practices are rapidly becoming the platinum standard in management and the benchmark for assessing operational risk.

The Public Company Accounting Reform and Investor Protection Act of 2002, commonly known as the Sarbanes-Oxley Act (SOX), was signed into law on July 30, 2002. SOX is one of the single most important piece of legislation affecting corporate governance, financial disclosure, and public accounting since the days of the Great Depression.

The Need to Combat Fraud

This is a true story. He was the brother-in-law of the owner of a small business. The business had grown steadily over the years, but still kept the same "Mom and Pop" mindset and business model that launched the venture years ago. Early on in the life of the company, his bookkeeping and accounting knowledge came in very handy for a business owner who had to watch every dime. His family connections made him even more valuable as the owner was very leery of allowing "outsiders" to handle the company's books. He did everything- bookkeeping, taxes – even annual audits of the company. No one else ever touched – or was allowed to touch - the books.

All was well until the day that the owner was notified by the IRS that his latest tax return was to be audited. As the owner began to examine the business's financial records, he was horrified to learn that this trusted family member had embezzled approximately $7 million over the past decade. Several months earlier, the owner had received a letter from the firm's insurance company declining to renew his crime policy. The company decided not to renew because the owner consistently refused to allow anyone other than his brother-in-law to handle the books or sign checks.

Sarbanes-Oxley Requirements and Best Practices for Small Businesses

SOX Requirements

Private companies (ones that are not publicly traded) are required to have a Whistleblower Protection Policy and a Document Preservation Policy. Both of these requirements serve to strengthen the company's infrastructure and help to safeguard it against waste, fraud and abuse.

Whistleblower Protection, however, is one provision from SOX that every business owner should be eager to put in place! Here are several reasons why this requirement benefits small businesses.

1. *Early detection of fraud or misappropriation* Detecting fraud or other serious conditions early on can save your business literally tens of thousands- if not millions- of dollars. It is the same reason why health insurance companies will gladly pay for cancer screening tests. Catching the disease in its early stages results in significant savings. Reward your whistleblowers!

2. Implementing a whistleblower protection policy will *give you an opportunity to discuss fraud candidly* with your employees and to motivate them to join you in a pro-active strategy to identify waste, fraud and abuse.

3. A well-crafted whistleblower protection policy should make it possible for you to *change any current interpersonal or business dynamics that need to be remedied*. The enforcement of a whistleblower protection policy can serve your business well in the event of any frivolous claims of wrongful termination or harassment.

4. The whistleblower policy provides you as the business owner with a *confidential means by which you can receive and investigate reports of waste, fraud and abuse.*

5. The policy lets everyone in the company know that *no one is above the law or entitled to misappropriate money, goods or other assets of the firm.*

Document Preservation Policy

Of the many factors that contributed to the Enron and Arthur Andersen scandals, the blatant attempts to destroy evidence by shredding documents was the basis for the SOX prohibition against destroying documents during an investigation or during legal proceedings. Sarbanes-Oxley compliance standards reflect what companies should have been doing all along! Having an integrated document management system ensures that important documents are stored in safe, accessible locations and backed-up on a daily basis. The core of any document management system is access and accountability. Having a solid document management program in place will introduce a higher level of efficiency, and accountability.

The written Document Preservation Policy should focus on these points:

*   *Describe what the Document Retention policy is* – and why it is required by law. It is important that employees understand that document preservation is a component of SOX that applies to all companies – not just publicly traded firms. The benefit of having an effective document preservation policy extends to improving the efficiency of archiving files and important documents. This saves time, improves effectiveness and reduces disorganization as this requirement applies to paper as well as electronic files.

*   *Identify what the new procedures are* that have emerged from the best practices around document preservation. Employee's need to understand how to be in compliance and what specific actions are required. They also need to understand the quality issues around these new behaviors and the scope of their new accountability.

- *Identify and explain what the obligations* of individual employees to ensure that your small business is in compliance. Requirements for individual employees should be presented in writing as part of their annual performance objectives or as part of their quarterly or semi-annual performance review. Because document preservation is probably a very new requirement in your company, it is particularly important to ensure that the guidelines are user-friendly.

- *Describe what is expected in terms of new behaviors* and procedures and the consequences for individual employees for failing to adhere to the new procedures. It is particularly important that management be prepared to carry out unpleasant consequences swiftly to send a strong message throughout the company.

Management needs to coordinate the activities in the implementation of a Document Preservation Policy and enforce the policies and procedures around document destruction. Since most of today's documents are stored in electronic format, implementing the specifics of the plan can be streamlined. The system you design for document storage, archives and retrieval must be logical and user-friendly. It is essential that everyone in the company –from the owner to senior management to the newest clerical employee understand what is expected. If an employee cannot understand what it is about, what is expected of them, and why they are being asked to do this, the probability of their compliance is low.

SOX Best Practices

In addition to the Whistleblower and Document Preservation requirements, a number of best practices have emerged from SOX legislation. The primary feature of these best practices is the creation of a work environment that discourages fraud.

Independent Auditor – The individual who conducts the company's audit should not be involved in any other services to the company such as tax preparation or consulting. If the company has a Board, the Executive Committee needs to appoint an Audit Committee whose role is to oversee the annual audit or financial review (for very small businesses) and to upgrade the financial literacy of management and corporate board if the small business has a Board.

Certified Financial Statements -The firm's management is ultimately accountable for the accuracy and integrity of the business's financial statements as well as the business's tax return. The company needs to ensure that the CEO or CFO can validate the accuracy of the business's financial statements.

Conflict of Interest Policy for board, management and key employees which facilitates greater focus on decision-making for the good of the business. Board members, management and key employees would be required to disclose on an annual basis whether they have any real or potential conflicts of interest based on their relationships and/or business interests.

Code of Ethics for board, management and employees that precludes any loans to directors, officers, management or employees of the business. The code of ethics should also address gifts or other potential "kickback" from vendors.

Internal Controls, particularly as these relate to financial operations, and compliance with all laws and regulations at the federal, state and local level. Internal controls, particularly as these relate to financial operations, and compliance with all laws and regulations at the federal, state and local level are at the heart of SOX compliance.

Segregation of Duties - Define employees' roles and responsibilities and ensure that duties are segregated, particularly as these relate to finance or handling of other assets. The purpose of this task structure is to ensure that no one is in a position to perpetrate fraud, embezzle or conceal their actions.

Recognize the role of technology in SOX compliance and best practices - SOX best practices recognize the pivotal role that IT plays not only in organizing data for operational application, but in how financial data is recorded and analyzed. IT plays a significant role in virtually every aspect of SOX requirements and best practices. Small businesses often overlook this aspect of management because their companies may only use standard software programs.

SOX best practices include the creation of a technology policy to safeguard the company's technology, internet access, email and other important technology. Be sure to have your legal counsel review and approve the language of your actual technology policy. The policy needs to include these talking-points:

- *Clearly state that all aspects of the small business's technology belongs to the small business.* There are NO expectations of personal privacy when using the small business's technology, including internet access and email.

- *Identify all of the small business's technology* – hardware and software including laptop computers, desktop computers, handheld devices such as PDAs and Blackberry, cell phones, internet access, email and all software programs purchased through the small business.

- *Institute a policy that requires the cleaning of hard drives prior to the recycling of PDAs or laptops.* Be aware that when electronic devices such as laptops or PDAs are "recycled" to another employee member, the "hard drive" of the device may still contain data, documents or transactions from the previous employee. It is important to institute a procedure to erase the hard drive once all of the documents have been extracted and stored according to your small business's Document Retention Policy.

- *Develop a policy on the storage and transportation of sensitive information out of your small business's facilities.* Published reports routinely describe scenarios of laptops being stolen that contained sensitive data. The same thing could happen to your small business if you store sensitive information about customers, clients, or employee on laptops that leave your premises.

All employees need to be briefed on the technology policy, receive a copy of the technology policy, and sign a letter stating that they have been briefed on the technology policy and pledge to comply with the policy.

Your Website

Your website is the electronic "face" of your company. The way in which it is designed, its features (which make it user-friendly – or not) and the content say important things about your company. Some small businesses utilize their websites to collect donations for charities they sponsor, sell merchandise, or respond to a global disaster. The small business's Document Preservation Policy should also include those "documents" which can be pages on the website such as:

- Your small business's annual financials if these would be part of an annual report.

- Documents that demonstrate SOX compliance and best practices such as your small business's Whistleblower Protection Policy and Document Preservation Policy.

- Reports, information about Management members, programs, annual reports, and financial reports.

Security is rapidly becoming one of the most significant challenges to websites – any website – small business or private sector. Small business websites need to have firewalls and encryption software to protect customer information and to ensure that transactions online with customers are secure.

Transparency at All Levels of Management

Management needs to insist that there are written procedures for filing travel and reimbursement claims and that these procedures are enforced – even by means of unannounced audits. Review current compliance activities and identify ways to reduce the number of key controls, increase the use of controls self-assessments and improve the overall control environment to better match compliance efforts to risk. Implement an ongoing fraud and risk management process to reduce losses. Improve the finance organization's capabilities.

The ROI of Best Practices

The implementation of SOX best practices pays dividends.

- *Governance* – If your small business has a board, compliance with Sarbanes-Oxley requirements and adaptation of best practices will make your board a more effective entity whose members understand and adhere to their fiduciary obligations and recognize their responsibility in governing the company. Additionally, good governance is an important factor in making the firm an attractive candidate for acquisition.

- *Accountability* – SOX best practices introduces higher levels of management and employee accountability including more reliable financial reports and other evidence of solid internal controls. Effective internal controls also serve as a deterrent to fraudulent activities and shrinkage of inventory.

- *Operations* - Effective protocols to ensure that the company remains in compliance with SOX and the company's "industry standards" and addresses future standards, particularly if the company is considering launching an IPO.

- *Marketing* - Better competitive positioning by making known that the company adheres to the SOX platinum standard in its operating practices.

- *Strategic Positioning* - Greater credibility and ability to attract necessary resources, be these in the form of high quality *independent* board members, sources of capital, business partners or other fund sources.

- *Thinking of Launching an IPO?* - If your company is thinking of launching an IPO, then the firm will have to show proof that it is in compliance with all SOX requirements. Putting the SOX best practices, whistleblower protection and document preservation policies into place will help position the company to come into compliance with all of the SOX requirements.

Final Checklist - How SOX Best Practices Can Help Your Company Combat Fraud

Your company can combat fraud, develop a more solid infrastructure and achieve a better competitive position by implementing SOX requirements and best practices. Here's a final checklist to begin the process.

Files organized in a more efficient manner- SOX document preservation policy establishes a more efficient system for managing files, databases and other forms of information.

Whistleblower protection policy encourages early warning of waste, fraud or abuse – This SOX requirement is probably the most effective method of detecting waste, fraud and abuse – if you frame it correctly.

Internal controls in place to standardize procedures- have solid internal controls, policies and procedures to introduce a standardized approach to operations and administration. Good internal controls are an active deterrent to fraudulent activities which can drain your company of money and materials.

IT systems integrated - or in process of being integrated - to support internal controls. Developing solid internal controls begins with ensuring that your IT system is designed to meet your company's size and needs. The money you spend to ensure that your IT framework will support the necessary internal controls is a solid investment for your company's growth and sustainability.

Ensuring that financials are accurate -The IRS and other public agencies now hold CFOs and/or other senior management criminally liable for veracity of financials and tax returns.

Summary

The best practices that have emerged from SOX legislation offer small businesses the means by which they can strengthen their internal controls, improve governance and become more pro-active in reducing the potential for waste, fraud and abuse. SOX best practices also facilitate changing the work environment to improve efficiency, reward transparency and provide employees with a safe and secure method to report waste, fraud and abuse. One of the most challenging paradigm changes that must occur in small business today is the role of the whistleblower. To punish a whistleblower is akin to disconnecting the firm's security system because you don't like the sound of the alarm ringing. Whistleblowers whose reports save the company time, money and embarrassment should be given a generous reward!

SOX best practices are the platinum standard in management today. These best practices can be fully implemented regardless of the size of your company. Improvement of internal controls, strengthening governance and protecting individuals who discover waste, fraud and abuse are the transformation elements that give your business the solid footing it will need to move to the next level.

Dr. Peg Jackson *is a leading authority on risk management, strategic and contingency planning and Sarbanes-Oxley compliance. She focuses her consulting work on designing strategies for nonprofits to strengthen their infrastructure and solidify their competitive positioning. Several of her texts on risk management, business continuity planning and Sarbanes-Oxley compliance have earned critical acclaim, and her latest work,* **Reputational Risk Management***, was released this year. She earned a doctorate in public administration (DPA) from Golden Gate University and holds the professional designation of Chartered Property and Casualty Underwriter (CPCU).*

23 Employment Dispute Resolution

Making the Best Out of a Bad Situation

By Mic Puklich

Over the course of the past few years, I have seen hundreds of books and articles on managing people and avoiding employment disputes. While many of these authors provide basic "good" information, it is important to note that avoiding any chance of an employment dispute will only become possible when people learn how to manage, predict and control human behavior. This is about as likely as Charlie Brown finally kicking a football. The simple fact is that as long as people associate and interact with one another, there is a possibility of a dispute. The trick, or art, is to be aware and ready.

By way of background, I am not an expert in human behavior. In fact, most of the time I do not even understand people. I am a lawyer. A lawyer who, for the past 15 years, has spent the majority of his working life dealing with employment disputes. Over the course of these years I have counseled individuals and small to mid size employers on a variety of employment disputes. I have tried numerous employment cases in both State and Federal Courts as well as multiple arbitration forums across the United States. I have observed and been involved with the problems and the issues on both sides (employer and employee), and saw firsthand what "could have" and "should have" been done to control or manage an employment dispute. It is with this background and experience that I have come to learn a few helpful "tips" that, although not universally applicable, are good points to consider if you find your-self in the unfortunate situation of an employment dispute.

I Am What I Do

A majority of people, right or wrong, define themselves in large part by their job. When you think about it, this should not be sur-prising. The typical American worker works between 40-50 hours per week - excluding the approximate 56 hours per week of sleep. Work is the single most time consuming activity in a person's life. It should, therefore, come as no surprise to most people that work is a big part of who they are. If you doubt this, simply think about the past introductions you have observed or been involved in and ask yourself these questions: what is the most common question asked during a first encounter, and what do people want to know? The answer is -- what do you do for a living? Simply put, work is important to people, and this fact cannot not be ignored. I have observed that the biggest reason employment disputes arise is be-cause somebody believes that they are underappreciated or under-valued. I have never been involved in a case where an employee felt valued yet saw fit to sue his/her employer.

Rule 1: Apply the golden rule at work; treat others as you would like to be treated.

How to apply the rule? Adopt polices that express your desire to treat others fairly. First, all employers should adopt an Equal Opportunity Policy. Some people will scoff at the idea of "equal opportunity." This is because it oftentimes gets confused with "af-firmative action," but the two are different. An Equal Employment Opportunity Employer is committed to complying with those laws that make certain forms of discrimination are illegal. All employers should be equal opportunity employers and should have a writ-ten statement indicating such. Affirmative Action Employers are those companies that are required by local, state or federal laws, to prepare and implement written affirmative action plan(s) for hiring/tracking minorities, women, disabled employees, Vietnam era veterans, and special disabled veterans. Only certain employers are required, in certain circumstances, to be affirmative action employers.

Second, if you are an employer and you do not have an employment handbook -- get one -- and make sure all of your employees receive a copy. The handbook should include information such as: (1) policies prohibiting sexual harassment, discrimination and retaliation; (2) a defined reporting structure - containing multiple complaint avenues for an individual to bring complaints or concerns; (3) policies relating to medical leave, sick time, jury duty, vacation, holidays and other leaves of absence (note: if you are an FMLA – covered employer you must include information regarding FMLA entitlements and employee obligations in your handbook); (4) a statement that the handbook does not create a contract and can be modified by the employer at any time (note: if there is no contractual disclaimer, under certain circumstances, a handbook may create an employment contract); (5) a statement that employment is at-will; (6) if the employee is subject to a commission structure, address when and how they will be paid and what, if anything, they will be paid if they leave or are terminated. Be sure to note that the commission structure may be changed or modified at the employer's discretion; (7) have the employee sign an acknowledgment that they received and understand the handbook; and (8) an equal opportunity statement.

Keep in mind that employers cannot pick and choose which laws to follow, even if they overlap. They must comply with all federal, state, and local laws that are applicable, even if the laws have different legal standards for regulating behavior in the workplace. Sometimes that means employers need to combine the laws and apply the provisions of each that are the most favorable to the employees.

As a result, employers must be certain that employee handbooks and other published policies are appropriately written based on the laws applicable to the different jurisdictions in which they are used. Multistate employers face particular challenges because it must also be determined whether to apply the federal, state, and local laws specific to each location or whether to combine the laws of all the jurisdictions and apply them uniformly across the board.

Alternatively, an employer may decide to write policies that apply a combination of the laws in every location while writing other policies more narrowly. For example, it could be very expensive for an employer to apply daily overtime standards in every state in which it has employees instead of only in those where it is required. On the other hand, it may be easier and more consistent with the corporate culture to apply the broader protections of some state and local discrimination laws in all locations in which a company does business.

The federal government and most states have informative web sites intended to help you figure out which laws apply. It is a good idea to check those web sites and then talk with human resources and legal counsel about the appropriate scope of application.

Should Have Done Something About the Chicken

Once upon a time a family moved from the city to the country. One night the family was robbed. The robbers broke into the barn and took a chicken. The family, upon noticing the theft, convened a meeting amongst themselves to decide what to do. After debate, they decided that since it was only a chicken, they would do nothing. Later that week the robbers returned and took a cow and a horse. The family again convened and, although upset and somewhat worried, decided that since nobody was hurt, they would do nothing. A few days passed and, while they were sleeping, the robbers broke into the house, took heirlooms and in the course of the robbery injured the family members. Upon convening to discuss the events the family members began to debate what to do. The family was upset and began talking about getting a security system, patrolling the homestead, and bringing in help. What to do? As they pondered this question, the mother finally spoke, "I don't know what to do now, but next time we are going to do something about the chicken."

It is easy to ignore problems, but they rarely go away. It is also much easier to deal with a stolen chicken than a catastrophic injury. Address employment issues before they grow out of control. In addressing issues, make sure that you document, document, and document your actions. It is difficult to overstate the need for documentation. As a clever quote that I heard some time ago uniquely put it, "Documentation is like sex, when it is good, it is very, very good; and when it is bad, it is better than nothing." Documentation is important for a variety of reasons: it brings concerns to the employee's attention; it highlights the importance of the issue to the employee; it formally alerts the employee to the issue and provides the employee an opportunity to improve; and it eliminates the "surprise" element (unless informed to the contrary, most people believe they are good performers). In creating documentation, keep the following in mind: be accurate, treat all employees equally, detail the facts, and avoid conclusions. Remember that most employment lawsuits arise out of terminations where the employee claims he/she was fired for unlawful or discriminatory reasons and the employer claims he/she was fired because of performance or disciplinary problems. With respect to documentation, keep these basic rules in mind:

- Maintain a contemporaneous record.
- Define the problem or issue.
- Explain the effect of the problem or issue on your organization.
- Be accurate in your accounts.
- Use precise time frames.
- Refer to specific instances or a pattern of conduct.
- Be fair to the employee.
- Explain your position clearly.
- Know the facts.
- Spell out the consequences.
- Permit input from the employee.
- Document, document and document.

The Law

The law is always subject to change. What may be legal today may be illegal tomorrow. With that caveat, most non-union employees are "at-will", which means that the employer can terminate the employee at any time and without any reason. While this general statement is true, it is subject to a variety of exceptions that drastically limit the employer's right to take any adverse action against an employee. There are four general areas to be aware of when faced with an employment dispute:

1. The laws prohibiting discrimination. It is illegal for an employer to take any adverse action against an employee based on the employee's race, color, creed, religion, sex, national origin, and marital status, status with regard to public assistance, membership or activity in a local commission, disability, sexual orientation or age.

2. There are a number of laws which prohibit taking action against an employee because they engaged in a legally protected activity. This encompasses the body of law generally referred to as "Whistleblowing." Whistleblowing or laws prohibiting retaliation include protection for those who report violations of the law, report or oppose a discriminatory practice, participate in a governmental investigation and/or refuse to engage in an activity that violates the law or the person believes, in good faith, violates the law.

3. A valid contract between an employer and employee may void the at-will relationship. Generally, whether or not a contract exists is pretty straightforward; however, in the employment context it is a bit more complicated. Documents such as offer letters, employee handbooks, personnel policies, and compensation plans may, under certain circumstances, create valid agreements. Tip for employers: make sure all of your documentation contains language noting that employment is "at-will."

4. The broad array of statutory laws may provide protection for an employee. For example, the Family Medical Leave Act, Sarbanes-Oxley and State Workers' Compensation Acts specifically prohibit an employer from taking adverse action

against an employee for exercising right(s) provided for under the acts.

In summary, if you have a dispute, make sure that you are following the law. The law is not always "common-sense;" in fact, some of it is counter-intuitive. If you fail to follow the law and your dispute turns into litigation, it can be very costly. Research compiled by the Jury Verdict Research Series indicates that the average wrongful termination compensatory loss is $532,016; sexual harassment compensatory loss averages $120,702; and work-related gender discrimination is averaging $501,622. These amounts do not include legal fees which historically have ranged from $50,000 to $1 million per claim. Throw on top of this, the cost of management time and the general cost of not being able to focus on your business, and the costs are staggering. Right or wrong, employment litigation is not an uncommon occurrence. During the past forty years employers have seen a steady rise in the volume of employment related litigation as Congress has passed a series of laws (Title VII, Age Discrimination in Employment Act, Americans with Disabilities Act and others) giving employees new legal rights and the ability to enforce those rights in court. In 1991, Congress expanded the types of employment cases tried to juries and broadened the types of damages that employees can recover. Since then, employment litigation in federal courts has increased nearly 300 percent, and state courts have experienced a similar rise in claims. The bottom line, be prepared, take your time, and do a fair examination of the particular facts in dealing with employment disputes. If you do not know the law or are unsure, contact a professional.

Policy, Procedure and Knowledge

One of the most common mistakes employers make is in the application of its policies and procedures. Generally speaking, employers should have policies and procedures for most common matters. As discussed earlier in this chapter, if you are an employer and you don't have an employment handbook … get one. Have it reviewed by a professional and make sure that all of your employees receive a copy.

Given the exceptions to the "at-will" rule, it is common for an employee to fall within some protected classification. If the employer treats a "protected class employee" different than a person who is not within the same protected class, questions concerning why the action was taken are bound to arise. When questions arise, the likelihood of a dispute - or litigation - increases. Consistent application of policies and procedures helps reduce the perception that somebody was treated unfairly or differently. This, in turn, reduces the likelihood of a dispute.

My single most important piece of advice for you – be honest. I know that sounds cliché and I do not intend for it to come across as a moral mandate. Among the most contentious disputes in which I have been involved, are those where the employer identified one reason for the adverse action at the time it was taken, and then switched his/her reason for the action at a later date. The "I didn't want to hurt your feelings, so I lied to you before, but now that you are suing me, I am going to tell you the truth," defense has its obvious flaws, both legally and factually. Disputes happen. If you find yourself in a dispute, lawful decisions are always easier to defend when they are made and communicated honestly.

Conclusion

This Chapter is meant to provide an overview of basic employment law principles. It is by no means a "bible" or shield that will protect you from liability. If you have specific questions, call a lawyer – most of them are good people.

Mic Puklich is an attorney who practices primarily in the areas of employment, civil rights, and business litigation. He has successfully represented hundreds of individuals and numerous corporations in a wide variety of litigation in both federal and state courts. Mic obtained the largest recovery awarded against the FAA in an employment matter, co-counseled on a $1.6 million jury verdict in a condemnation trial, and, in 2005, obtained the largest verdict in the State of Minnesota for a workers' compensation retaliation case. Mic is a member of the Million Dollar Advocates Forum, comprised of attorneys who have obtained settlements and trial verdicts in excess of $1 million, and was named a Top 40 Attorney in Employment Law. Mic graduated, magna cum laude, from William Mitchell College of Law.

About Business Expert Publishing

Business Expert Publishing, The Business Book Publisher™, is a division of the Business Expert Webinars group in cooperation with 3 Palms Publishing Group. BEP was founded by Lee Salz (www.BusinessExpertWebinars.com) and Jeb Blount (www.Sales-Gravy.com) with the mission to publish relevant and timely business books by respected business experts.

The *Business Expert Guide* series is designed to help business leaders with specific business challenges in an easy to read and easy to implement format.

To learn more about Business Expert Publishing visit: http://www.businessexpertpublishing.com.

Recent titles from Business Expert Publishing

- *Managing The Black Hole: The Executives Guide to Software Project Risk* by Gary Gack - ISBN: 1935602012

- *Reputational Risk Management: The Essential Guide to Protecting Your Reputation in Crisis Situations* by Peggy M. Jackson - ISBN: 1935602020

- *Stop Speaking For Free! The Ultimate Guide to Making Money with Webinars* by Lee B. Salz & Jenny L. Hamby - ISBN: 1935602039

www.ingramcontent.com/pod-product-compliance
Lightning Source LLC
Chambersburg PA
CBHW031807190326
41518CB00006B/226